45 RPM
(Recollections Per Minute)

—m—

The Morrell Archives Volume 3

Dave Morrell

Credits:
Cover Design by Jack Snyder
Thanks to Brenda Hanson, Ivan Kral, Bruce Somerfeld, Len Scaffidi, John Ogle, Mario Casciano, Worthy Patterson and Richard Neer.
Special thanks to Judi Kerr for her continued support and love.
Copyright © 2017 Dave Morrell All rights reserved.

ISBN: 1545035385
ISBN 13: 9781545035382

Table of Contents

Preface 1975-1980 v

1. "America vs. John Lennon" (Round Two) 1
2. The 17th Annual Grammy Awards Show 7
3. Paul McCartney Smokes A Doobie 11
4. Phil Spector 15
5. "Atlantic Crossing" – Rod Stewart 19
6. "What Is Hip?" – Taxi Driver 23
7. "EXTRA! - MORRELL TO RCA: FAB FOUR TO WB: GOOD LUCK DAVE" 27
8. Nipper – RCA 29
9. "What's A Guy Like You?" 33
10. WNEW FM – The Winds Have Shifted In Our Favor 35
11. "Coney Island Baby" – Lou Reed 39
12. John Denver 43
13. "Station To Station" – David Bowie 45
14. Jefferson Starship – Central Park 49
15. Hall & Oates 51
16. The Big Bonus Bucks 53
17. Nashville 59

18. Elvis Presley 65
19. The Rumpdogs Are On The Phone 69
20. 20th Century Fox Records 73
21. Carly Simon 79
22. Arista..83
23. "Street Hassle" – Lou Reed 89
24. WABC Radio The Biggest And Greatest
    Station Of All Time 93
25. "Because The Night" - Patti Smith Group.......................97
26. The New Wonder Of The World 105
27. 1978 – Duly Noted..111
28. The Promotion Man 115
29. "Don't Cry Out Loud" – Melissa Manchester..............119
30. New York City's WNEW FM Top 25 Albums 1978 ...123
31. "(Wish I Could Fly Like) Superman" - Kinks...............127
32. 1979 – Nitty Gritty..129
33. "Déjà Vu" – Dionne Warwick 139
34. The Conference Call "We're A Million Short On
    Manilow!"..143
35. "Hooray For Hollywood!" 147

Preface
1975-1980

Foot on the gas, clean windshield, the punks are up ahead, CBGB's has another show at 4am, Disco music, clubs, Quaaludes, Cuban heels, bongs, uptown, downtown, midtown. Be at the scene, cover the shows, spread the music, but be in at 10am.

Bounce off Iggy Pop, Lou Reed, David Bowie, Patti Smith Group, too. Regroup and recalculate with Elvis, John Denver, The Four Seasons, All This and World War II!

The bunny was in the rear view mirror, Maria was in the dust, and Gord's Gold was on the turntable.

After high school I couldn't get anything going. Even with matches I couldn't start a fire. After a year of wearing out the heels on my boots, I stumbled and tripped into a warehouse for Warner Brothers Records on the outskirts of a town. It was full of albums and 8-tracks and cassettes. I knew I had to stay.

I picked and I packed. I counted and I shipped. I emptied trucks and I stuffed envelopes. I went to sales and promotion meetings and spoke out loud about all the cool stuff we had to send out. We sent records and buttons and t-shirts too!

They sent me to concerts. They took me backstage with them. They introduced me to artists and took us all out to dinners. I was in awe. They loved being nice to the New York guy. It all worked out.

They asked me to promote records to radio stations. These were radio stations I grew up listening to. I always heard the DJ's, but didn't even know what many of them looked like.

The men I met cajoled muscled and worked their mojo.

There was "Midnight at the Oasis," "Sundown," "Tin Man," "Black Water," "Another Park, Another Sunday," "Bungle in the Jungle," and more. There was Frank Sinatra, Neil Young, Black Sabbath, Faces, Procul Harum, Badfinger, Blazing Saddles and The Exorcist, too!

I was eating three meals a day and not gaining an ounce. I was out all night and worked all day. I got mauled driving to the big apple over bridges and under tunnels.

We owned the airwaves. We partied hearty and nobody got hurt.

I met John Lennon and low and behold he liked me.

Up ahead was country, disco, r&b, pop and rock. Skip the record and begin the beguine.

Ram on, rock on, read on and don't forget to PLAY LOUD and HAVE FUN!

Chapter 1
"America vs. John Lennon" (Round Two)

Scene One: John Lennon's Bed - September 1974

John Lennon was looking my way. Between his fingers was a lit joint and he handed it to me. Derek Taylor and May Pang were there too. John was smiling and giggling and sitting like a Buddha on his bed, obviously in a good mood. I inhaled, looked at him and then closed my eyes. The pot was like a chisel cracking the rocks in my skull that formed over a lifetime and became cold and hidden with the abilities to break free. Man I was getting stoned!

I could sense commotion around me while my eyes were closed. John had just been showing us his new album, "Walls & Bridges," and how the cover jacket had flaps that opened & closed with him wearing different glasses and making different faces. John was extremely pleased it turned out so well. He took the vinyl out and walked on his bed over to the stereo to play it.

With the volume up and John showing off the finished goods, he accidently played side two first! He dropped the needle and a burst of guitar over a dreamlike string arrangement filled the room. Then John's quaalude spacey voice came on and began to sing, "Soooo long ago, was it in a dream? Was it just a dream? I know, yes I know, it seemed so very real, seemed so real to me." The sound was intoxicating. It's a moment you never forget even if you're smoking pot!

Then May shouted, "I'm on it, too!"

I was surprised to hear that and thought maybe she played a tambourine or a triangle, but sure enough, a minute and a half into the song, she was whispering "John" in a sultry voice over and over. It fit the song beautifully.

I told John I loved the track. It was wonderful. I told him I couldn't wait to hear it on the radio. He told me it was called "#9 Dream" and he said the number nine was his favorite number.

Over the next three months John was out promoting "Walls & Bridges." He turned up at WNEW-FM to be on the air with his collection of old records. He went up for a photo opportunity at WABC. He played at Elton John's Thanksgiving night show at Madison Square Garden and blew the roof off the place. His first single, "Whatever Gets You Thru The Night," became his only #1 single in Billboard in his lifetime. And as the New Year began, John's own composition from "Sgt. Pepper's Lonely Hearts Club Band," "Lucy In the Sky With Diamonds," was #1 on the charts by Elton John featuring John singing with him.

It was a tremendous time to be around John Lennon.

January 1975

It was time for a follow up to "Whatever Gets You Thru The Night" and John chose "#9 Dream" to be the second single from the album. Meanwhile at WB, it was also time to follow up "Tin Man" by America with a new single so they chose "Lonely People," which was actually written as a positive response to the Beatles "Eleanor Rigby" and produced by George Martin to boot.

In the past year we were placing WB artists on WABC for the first time ever. Artists like Maria Muldaur, Leo Sayer, America and even Jethro Tull were now getting Top 40 airplay.

It was time for another royal battle to achieve airplay and head to the top of the charts.

As the America vs. John Lennon battle was about to go down, WB had another hit coming up quick. It was the Doobie Brothers "Black Water," which originally was the b-side of "Another Park, Another Sunday." It turns out a radio guy started playing "Black Water" and was getting phenomenal audience reaction.

It was the end of the month when WABC, the powerhouse Top 40 radio station in New York, added both America and John Lennon records at the same time. John had the upper edge being a Beatle, living in NYC and having a strong profile. America hadn't been around the New York area often and most people didn't know the individual members' names.

On the retail side, white soft-core records like Bread, America, the Eagles, and Harry Chapin were a tough sell for single records and never had the boost or combined total that R&B and Dance records had in NYC. At WB we'd have to work hard and smart. The national numbers were coming in and we had to be prepared.

America vs. John Lennon (Round 2)

On January 28th, "Lonely People" was added at #39 on the WABC playlist. Lennon's "#9 Dream" was also added at a close #30. We needed to follow this up with a good week of at least a two-point jump.

The following week (February 4) WABC added the Doobie Brothers, "Black Water," at a super high debut of #22. That same week "#9 Dream" fell backwards to #32 while "Lonely People" got a whopping 10-point jump to #29!

WB was hot and firing on all cylinders. The salesmen were getting us those store reports we needed. The following week (February 11) was another huge shift with "#9 Dream" going from #32 to #12, while America shot up 12 points to go from #29 to #17. WB was happy we'd at least have a follow up Top 15 coming off their hit "Tin Man." The Doobie Brothers went backwards from #22 to #23. Over at our sales meeting, it was clear we needed to boost the sales reports on "Black Water."

We all got on the phones Monday to make sure we didn't lose WABC on the Doobie Brothers. By Tuesday, the results were in and they were terrific. The playlist for the week of February 19th showed the Doobie Brothers moving from #23 to the Top 10! (#10), while America went Top 15 (#15). John's record of "#9 Dream" went backwards from #12 to #19 but, hold the phone, they added a new John Lennon song from a rush-released new album, an oldie John recorded for his upcoming "Rock 'n' Roll" album called "Stand By Me." It was good, real good, but John didn't write it and wouldn't receive the royalties as he would for "#9 Dream." This new release might also kill off all the momentum that was built around "Walls & Bridges."

45 RPM (Recollections Per Minute)

For Capitol it was time to move on to promoting the "Rock 'n' Roll" album and abandoning the "Walls & Bridges" record.

As it turned out, "#9 Dream" went on to peak (fittingly) at #9 on the Billboard charts on February 22. Also interesting to note that John had produced Harry Nilsson's "Pussycats" album a few months before and came up with a great string arrangement for Harry Nilsson's version of "Many Rivers to Cross." John liked it so much that he took it back for his own song. Check it out sometime.

Capitol rush-released John's "Rock 'n' Roll" album on February 17th. The single, "Stand By Me," was sent to radio immediately and, amongst all the commotion and confusion, stalled at #20 on the Billboard singles chart.

John had also gotten back together with Yoko and they were about to re-emerge as a couple for the upcoming Grammys.

Chapter 2
The 17th Annual Grammy Awards Show

Scene Two: Uris Theatre - New York City

It was March 1, 1975 and the 17th Annual Grammy show was in New York City. I scored a ticket from WB and was very excited to attend. I didn't know what to expect, but the fireworks started as soon as I walked into the banquet for the guests.

John & Yoko were sitting together and everyone was stopping by to welcome them. I had to go over and say hello too. When John turned to look at me and shake hands, I noticed he was wearing a big silver pin on his jacket that read, in script, 'Elvis.' He said he was back together with Yoko. We smiled and I said, "Great pendent!" He laughed and said Yoko gave it to him. "She knows how much I love Elvis!" he said.

I mentioned the two-tone Elvis button he'd been wearing since his birthday back in October and he said it was tough taking that one off and putting the new one on. This new one was jewelry he said. The other was pure 1956!

For his 34th birthday party held over at the Record Plant East a few short months ago, I had given John an old antique Elvis button I had been wearing on all my jackets and sports coats at the time. I didn't know what else to give him. I was surprised how much he loved it. He had been wearing it everywhere until this evening.

He asked me what was happening and I reminded him about some Elvis TV shows he'd never seen. I knew he would dig them.

Back at his apartment a few months earlier we spoke about some rare Elvis TV appearances a friend had on 16 mm and John was looking forward to seeing them. I reminded him and he told me to write to him at the Dakota and put a little code on the envelope so he'd look at it. He told me the code and also told me he used it to send stuff to himself at the Dakota.

I told him how happy I was for him on his recent success and he stopped me to say he was working with Bowie! The first thing I said was "Gimme Some Truth" would be fantastic and he said, "How 'bout, "Across the Universe?" I asked him if it was his recording session or Bowie's and he said it was Bowie's. I couldn't wait to hear it! As it turned out John not only wrote "Across the Universe," but also had a hand in writing David Bowie's "Fame" from his new album about to come out called "Young Americans." "Fame" would become a #1 record in September.

It was 1975, the year Paul Simon and John handed out the Record of the Year award for "I Honestly Love You" by Olivia Newton John. Art Garfunkel surprised everyone by coming on stage and accepting the award.

45 RPM (Recollections Per Minute)

David Bowie was also there and gave the award for Best Rhythm & Blues by a female artist. It went to Aretha Franklin who promptly said, "This is so good I could kiss David Bowie!"

Paul McCartney won that year for Best Pop Group for "Band On The Run," but Paul wasn't present at the show to accept the award. Elvis won for Best Inspirational Performance with "How Great Thou Art."

The nominees for Album of the Year were Stevie Wonder's "Fulfillingness' First Finale," Elton John's "Caribou," John Denver's "Back Home Again," Joni Mitchell's "Court & Spark," and Paul McCartney and Wings "Band On The Run." Stevie won the award.

Chapter 3
Paul McCartney Smokes A Doobie

I was having fun getting records played and following the charts. Of course, if it was a battle with a Beatle, it really made it interesting for me.

WB was on fire! Over the past 12 months we had major WABC airplay on artists like Maria Muldaur, Todd Rundgren, America, Gordon Lightfoot, Leo Sayer and the Doobie Brothers.

"Black Water" by the Doobie Brothers was a Top 5 hit at WABC, and their follow up single, "Take Me in Your Arms (Rock Me a Little While)," was from a brand new album called "Stampede." It was a Motown cover that rocked hard.

Back at home, I installed two jukeboxes in the living room. Both were from the 50's and both sounded different. One of them had a big horn on top that gave it the brightness and bite. We had both boxes filled with old and new records. We'd pull up chairs and sit right in front of them listening to the warmth the tubes would bring to the vinyl.

Since I was working the singles at WB, I wanted to hear what they sounded like in a gin-mill setting where people would have to pay to hear them. We had these machines set up to play for free. We got so carried away, we installed a remote table counter top jukebox over the tub in the bathroom. After a tough day working in NYC there was nothing like smoking a joint, lighting the incense and candles, settling into a warm bath and playing your favorite songs on the old jukebox.

It got so nutty I had a few disconnected counter top jukeboxes and converted them into Rolodexes. I put peoples names and phone numbers in place of the song titles. I even gave a few away as Christmas gifts to key people.

At the same time as the Doobies, Paul McCartney and Wings released "Listen to What the Man Said," from his new album "Venus and Mars." It was another great song and, as far as I was concerned, a better song than his last single, "Junior's Farm."

I was up in the lobby at WABC when the Capitol promotion man arrived with the test pressing of Paul and Wings' new single. By now he knew I was a big Beatle nut and immediately told me he had no extra copies for my collection. He said he would try to get me one.

On June 3, WABC added both the Doobie Brothers "Take Me in Your Arms (Rock Me a Little While)" and Paul McCartney and Wings "Listen to What the Man Said." The Doobies came on the WABC playlist at #31, while Paul and Wings came on as a Hit Pick. The race to the top of the charts was on!

I was holding a slot in the jukebox for the Wings' promo single, but it never arrived from Capitol.

45 RPM (Recollections Per Minute)

The following week, June 10, the Doobies moved up to #28, while Paul and Wings came in at #31. At the top of the chart, holding down the #1 position, was "The Hustle" by Van McCoy.

The next week Frankie Valli took over #1 with "Swearin' To God," while the Doobies made a great 5 point jump to #23. Paul and Wings soared over the Doobies with an astonishing #31 to #12 move. We needed to get on the phones to make sure our retail reports were strong for the following week.

On June 24, "The Hustle" rebounded to #1 while the Doobies took a great 7 point jump to #16, and Paul and Wings slowed down and crawled from #12 to #11. We were on our way to the Top 15 and Paul was closing into the Top 10. Both records were performing like a true hit.

On July 1, WABC had Frankie Valli back at the coveted #1 position, while "Take Me in Your Arms (Rock Me a Little While)" had run its course. The single stalled nationally at #10, although the album made it to the Top 5. The Wings album, "Venus and Mars," made it to #1 and so did the single, "Listen to What the Man Said."

Paul McCartney smoked a Doobie when it came to leaving them in his exhaust.

The next Doobie Brothers album would feature a new lead singer, Michael McDonald.

Meanwhile, my friend Hood, who worked for the local concert promoter, and I went out to have dinner at a 50's juke joint in Montclair, NJ and when we walked in we saw a cool 1965 jukebox with rare record sleeves. It wasn't on or lit up so we figured it was a just being used as a display. Once we ordered our burgers and milkshakes music began to fill the room. We called the soda jerk over and asked him if it was that jukebox. He said no but that it did work.

He plugged it in and it came to life. It sounded like a speaker was blown and it needed repair. He told me it was for sale. I didn't want to hear that since I had no money and no room at the house but I took a minute and thought about it. I figured a broken jukebox like this was worth about $1500 and to repair it would be another $500.

The kid said the owner wanted $150.00 and it came with the records.

I asked Hood to loan me a $20 dollar bill for a hold on the machine. We'd be back in an hour.

We loaded it on to Hood's van and took it to a guy who I knew could fix the speakers. He charged me $50 and it was good as new.

Hood and I went through the records and picture sleeves and realized we hit a gold mine. I gave Hood whatever he wanted and we now had three jukeboxes at the house in Kearny, NJ.

Life was good! It was now time for Hood and Dave to smoke a Doobie!

Chapter 4
Phil Spector

"Morrell! Pack your bags and get to LA! We're going over to meet Phil Spector and hear some new music."

I couldn't believe what I was hearing. This was sensational news! "Be My Baby," by the Ronettes, was one of my first 45's and Phil produced it with his famous "wall of sound."

John Lennon had just released his "Rock 'n' Roll" album and Phil had produced some of the tracks. I was hoping to talk to him about the sessions and if there were any songs that weren't released or some jam sessions that may have taken place. I was getting excited to meet him in person. I was thinking about the "Let It Be" album he produced. I wanted to ask him about those Beatle tapes. Did he listen to everything the Beatles put on tape? My mind was spinning!

Phil signed a deal with WB Records to put music out and I was the NYC promotion man. I knew he'd identify with me and we'd get along great. But sometimes things don't work out that way.

For example, Sonny Bono was a promo man for Phil, and one time, in December 1964, he took Phil's newest single, "Walkin' in the Rain" by the Ronettes, to the hot Top 40 station in Los Angeles. The DJ he played it for was less than enthusiastic and even grimaced. Then he said, "It sounds kinda tired."

Sonny left the station to call Phil and give him the news. Phil picked up the phone and asked, "Am I making money?" Sonny told him they weren't going to add it right away.

"It didn't get on this week," Sonny said.

There was silence on Phil's end of the call.

Sonny was a goner.

Phil's first two songs for the new deal at WB flopped. One was by Cher called "A Woman's Story," and the other, "Dance, Dance, Dance," was by a band called Calhoon.

I didn't realize Phil just might be in a bad mood when we met him.

My boss at WB took a few members of the staff over to meet Phil in the recording studio. We all walked in and Phil was standing there with his bodyguard. Later they told me he had a bodyguard to make sure he didn't hurt himself!

Rather than being polite and welcoming, Phil went on a rant. He started screaming that we couldn't get Beatle records played in Liverpool. That none of us were any good. He said the Cher record was a hit that we blew. It was actually a stinker that never charted in the Billboard Hot 100.

After what seemed like forever yelling at us, my boss finally had enough. He took control.

"Hey Phil!" he barked. "Play the new music we came to hear or we're leaving!"

45 RPM (Recollections Per Minute)

Phil would have nobody talk down to him so he bellowed, "I'm not done! I wanna know what's happening with my records. I'm not playing anything 'til I get some answers!"

Phil was losing it. I was confused. I wanted a do over. I wanted to shake his hand and talk for a while and then play some cool music.

My boss couldn't take it any longer. He shouted, "Phil! You got 30 seconds to hit the play button or we're gone."

Phil look bothered. He stated flailing his arms and refused to hit the play button.

My boss said, "That's it! Let's go!"

We all got behind my boss and single filed our way out of there.

I never did meet Phil, or shake his hand, but I did get an unexpected letter from him that included a button that had his famous saying, BACK TO MONO. The letter made me laugh. I had no idea why he sent it to me. It was dated March 19, 1975 and it read:

Dear Dave,

I'd like to thank you for all that you've done on behalf of Warner/Spector product.

Warmest personal regards,

Phil Spector

I thought maybe one day Phil would come to NY and stop by the office, but that never happened. In fact, nothing ever happened at Warner/Spector.

Something so right just turned out so wrong. Phil never had a hit while with WB.

Chapter 5
"Atlantic Crossing" – Rod Stewart

Rod has a gravel voice that rips the paint off a masterpiece and leaves you shattered. Whether Rod was singing the blues, or crying a ballad, it all had an impact on me. Songs he chose, like "Mandolin Wind," "I Would Rather Go Blind," and "Country Comforts" were the songs that filled my bedroom, my car, my speakers and my headphones.

I was a fan. I wished my hair could look like that. I wished I had the clothes he had. I'm not sure if it was Rod Stewart or the New York Dolls that made me give in and buy my first pair of platform shoes with a huge five-inch heel. Man, I was a dreamer.

Rod Stewart came on our scene after I stopped putting posters up in my bedroom. A few years earlier Rod would have been up there along with Marlon Brando, Bridget Bardot, the Beatles, the Rollin' Stones and Bob Dylan. I had the peace sign and a few others in traditional day-glow black light too.

I'd been a big fan before Rod hit it big with his smash solo hit 'Maggie May." My friends and I made sure to line up to buy tickets to see Rod in concert. One time the Faces played at the old Stanley Theatre in Jersey City, NJ. It was a huge old place and after the first show Rod told the audience we could all stay for the late show free if we just went up to the balcony. We had us a real good time until I went to get the car.

The lot was closed and I was locked in. I didn't mention I had borrowed my sister's car and knew she'd kick my ass. After a long fun evening, I had to bust my ass to catch a bus and a train and a long walk home, only to have to do it all over early the next morning.

I told my sister I got lucky with some girl and spent the night in a no-tell motel. I told her thanks and that I'd have the car back by noon. Whew, I was off the hook.

One day at work while making phone calls, I heard from the hallway Rod Stewart was coming to America. WB signed him and he was coming to promote his new record. I couldn't believe my luck. I loved Rod. I saw him live many times and I bought all his records. I was thrilled.

He teamed up with Tom Dowd and they put together an album called "Atlantic Crossing." Rod went down to Muscle Shoals Sound Studios to make the new record. This was a new beginning for him and WB records. This time instead of using his band, the Faces, Tom Dowd hooked him up with the Memphis Horns and a few of the Booker T and the MG'S guys.

WB was springing for lunch to launch the album. It was at an expensive private room off the hotel where Rod, his girlfriend Britt Ekland who was a (James) Bond girl and once married to Peter Sellers, and Rod's manager Billy Gaff were staying.

We invited all the press, radio, trades, and sales folks.

45 RPM (Recollections Per Minute)

I sat at the table with the WABC radio folks. The program director and music director came along with a few of the DJ's.

Rod came sweeping in and met all the WB crew first. Then we took him around to each table and introduced him while taking photographs.

Rod was dressed to the nines wearing an incredible, impeccable Seville Row custom-made suit. Rock stars in suits were always a sight to behold. I'd seen Alice Cooper in a three-piece red plaid suit at the Plaza Hotel a few years earlier and that was mind blowing.

When it was time for Rod to sit down, he chose to sit with us at the WABC table. We had a ball. We laughed our way through lunch. One of the DJ's told him a funny story about Simon & Garfunkle. He said, "Imagine the face on the Producer when these two kids from Queens came into a New York City recording studio and asked if they could record the sounds of silence."

Rod laughed and then told us about his new single, "Sailing" He was going to dress up like a sailor for a photo session the following day on a Schooner and sail the Hudson River. He told us we could come!

When we were done I told Rod about the show I'd seen in Jersey City, NJ. He not only remembered it, he recalled what clothes he was wearing at the time. I was delighted!

After lunch and all the farewells Rod invited me upstairs to his hotel suite. His manager was there and so was Britt who was gorgeous. Rod ordered a fine bottle of champagne and we kicked back and talked about all the radio people he knew and who we were going to do interviews with over the next few days. Rod was sensational. He loved talking and promoting his new record.

When it was time to leave, Rod took a towel and wrapped up the glass we drank from and handed it to me. "Good luck getting out of the hotel with a stolen glass and towel son!" he said. I couldn't wait to start calling radio stations and telling them Rod has a great new album that's a must hear!

Chapter 6
"What Is Hip?" – Taxi Driver

Crazy Shirley was the name we gave her. She was tall, blonde and beautiful and told us she was an actress and model. She'd hang out at the WB townhouse during the day. So did the actress Elisabeth Ashley. Actors had a lot of time off between movies and they knew the people in the music business had all the cool parties and concert tickets. It was a natural fit.

Shirley Kuhn was her real name but she went by the stage name of Billie Perkins. She was either living with or married to Ian McDonald from the band King Crimson. Shirley was always with us and great fun to be around. One day we were walking together by the Ed Sullivan Theatre on Broadway and directly next door was an old gin mill. She pointed through the glass and said, "Look, that's me!" and sure enough it was her official 8x10 photograph in a frame, autographed, in the center of the window. She was so proud and I was thrilled for her. She'd often tell me about her dreams to be in a movie. It was about to come true.

She told me she was up for a role as a prostitute in a tiny film that was being shot in the East Village. I told her she was nuts! I told her to be careful and not to take her clothes off for any of these people. She told me their names but they didn't stick. In fact, after hearing them, I immediately couldn't remember them. They were new to me and some were hard to say.

Up at the WB townhouse our favorite band at the moment was Tower Of Power and they were playing that evening at the Bottom Line. This was a show everyone in the building was looking forward to. You couldn't go by someone's office without hearing the band. They were that hot.

I invited Shirley, who I called Billie, and she told me she'd be working on the movie that day and could I meet her downtown on location. She said it was a small movie with a just a few actors and then rattled off their names. I never heard of any of them.

I asked her if all the streets were blocked off with the cops all around directing traffic. She laughed and said don't worry about it, I could come down and park anywhere.

She told me she was down on 13th Street between Second and Third Avenues. She said they were filming in front of #204. I got in my car and headed downtown. I found a spot to park and went looking for her. I expected some kind of Hollywood set but there was nothing but a Checker cab double-parked.

I found her and got her attention. She was just finishing and I asked her if she was in costume and needed to change. "No," she said, "these are my street clothes and also the clothes I wore in the scene." My first thought was, man this is a cheap movie!

She introduced me to a guy running things whose name was Marty. He was a great guy and when I told him we were heading to see a concert he told me he filmed and worked on the Woodstock movie. I loved his story and asked him to come with us or meet us there. He said he'd think about it. Then I met a guy named Bobby who I'd never seen before. He was playing the guy driving the big Checker cab.

The movie was "Taxi Driver" and Billie's friends were Martin Scorsese and Robert De Niro.

Years later when Marty premièred "The Last Waltz" he invited Shirley to be his date.

The Bottom Line was a club where I'd seen tons of singer songwriters but to see a sea of horns blowing in unison was insane, fun and crazy. The band held us right in the palms of their hands. With the great Lenny Williams on vocals, they worked thru "Squib Cakes," "Down to the Nightclub," and the classic "What is Hip?"

Down at the Bottom Line you could feel the heat. The vibes from the audience were infectious. Everyone knew each song. The joint was hoppin' and nobody was sitting down. The band even stormed into the audience. Music was all around me and I was with a pretty girl who was sitting on top of the world. Life was great!

We were soul vaccinated that hot summer evening.

I took Shirley back to the townhouse and used my key to gain entrance to the private locked 5th floor Penthouse where we usually threw all our parties.

The next thing we knew it was sunny out and the morning had broken.

It's amazing to go back to that movie and remember the day and night so vividly.

Chapter 7
"EXTRA! - MORRELL TO RCA: FAB FOUR TO WB: GOOD LUCK DAVE"

Big changes were happening all around me. My closest partners were leaving WB. I was working the WB singles and Mike Shavelson was working the WB albums. Mike was hoping for a national position in the home office and when it didn't pan out he left WB to join Epic Records in a national position. He'd go on to break the band Cheap Trick.

Worthy Patterson, who brought me out of the warehouse and made me a promotion man, was leaving, too. He was offered a position to become the head of promotion at RCA Records. Worthy said he'd be the first black head of all promotion, including Country music.

Besides losing my closest allies, WB was about to close the cool four-story townhouse in Midtown and move us to a corporate building over in Rockefeller Center a few blocks away. The pizzazz was gone.

One day while working on the upcoming Fleetwood Mac tour and a new single by the Four Seasons called "Who Loves You," my phone rang. It was Worthy. He wanted to make me the NY promotion man at RCA and work under him. I had no idea what was going on over at RCA since I never followed them, but I couldn't resist the temptation to work with Worthy again. He wasn't a screamer. He gave you some rope to work with and always encouraged you to succeed. He was wise beyond his age and was firmly rooted with no ego. I was going to follow him. The raise for a kid my age was good, too!

I told everyone at WB I was leaving and, like Worthy and Mike before me, WB didn't counter offer anything to keep us. The NY office threw me a fun party that included a fake newspaper with the headline:

"EXTRA! - MORRELL TO RCA: FAB FOUR TO WB: GOOD LUCK DAVE"

I laughed!

Funny thing. After all the talk about WB going after John Lennon and Paul McCartney who were now free agents, WB signed George Harrison. I was happy for all my friends who'd go on to work with George. I'd get to work with Paul in 10 years when he came back to Capitol after signing with Columbia.

Chapter 8
Nipper – RCA

RCA came courting me and boy did they have a deal for a 22 year old kid. First I met the Human Resources guy and he asked me if I spent around $200.00 a week on taking programmers out to eat. I said, "That sounds about right." He told me I'd be getting a checkbook with fifty weeks worth of checks that were good for $200.00 each. I was told to cash one each Monday and use the money to take the DJs out to eat, plus expenses out of that for cabs and that kind of stuff. The guy told me I'd be returning all the money that wasn't used. Hmmmm for some reason it would turn out I'd spend more than the $200.00 and RCA would owe me money. It was a wonderful world.

On top of that, I would be getting a brand new 1976 Malibu all hopped up with a quad sound system, racing stripes and a base paint of silver with a beautiful transparent blue to make it a head turner. Of course in New York, you didn't even need a car. In the first year at the company I didn't put 500 miles on the car.

They were even paying more that I ever could dream of and I didn't need it to live on. I had free records, free tickets to shows, expense account, car, and I was living with a bunch of friends who were all in the music business.

When I left WB I never realized there would be no more pop singles on WABC from America, Maria Muldaur, Gordon Lightfoot or James Taylor.

I happened to be at the right time and the right place when it came to James Taylor and his wonderful career. I was such a big Beatle fan I was more interested in talking to James about Apple and working with Peter Asher (Peter & Gordon) than I was about his current recordings. I was lucky since I got to work the Top 5 hit "How Sweet It Is (To Be Loved By You)," a cover of the Marvin Gaye song. James had struggled with the previous four singles spanning two years. 1973's "One Man Paradise," and "Hymn," off the album "One Man Dog." "Daddy's Baby," and "Walking Man," followed those singles in 1974 from the "Walking Man" album.

After "How Sweet It Is (To Be Loved By You)," it was back to non-Top 40 hits like "Mexico," "Shower the People," "Everybody has the Blues," "You Make it Easy," and "Woman's Got to Have It."

With Gordon Lightfoot's smash "If You Could Read My Mind, " from 1970, there was a four-year dry spell until 1974. Then after a great run with "Sundown," "Carefree Highway," "Rainy Day People," and "The Wreck of the Edmund Fitzgerald," he failed to catch the attention of the key Top 40 programmers.

Maria Muldaur was coming off a huge album and the hit "Midnight at the Oasis," but was unable to score with the

45 RPM (Recollections Per Minute)

follow up "I'm a Woman," "Gringo En Mexico," and "Sad Eyes."

For America, after their spectacular debut, in 1972, with "A Horse With No Name," they followed it up with "I Need You," "Ventura Highway," and in 1973 had "Muskrat Love." By the time I got to work with them in 1974, they had huge hits with "Tin Man," "Lonely People," "Sister Golden Hair," and "Daisy Jane." After that they didn't score anything else at WABC.

People were making fun of RCA at the time. One of the promotion guys asked me if I knew the difference between RCA and the Titanic. He said the Titanic had better bands.

I knew it would be a challenge since I spent my first three years inside WEA and knew the ins and outs of the organization but with Worthy at the helm I felt confident. Looking back I had no need to worry. We broke four bands and had the biggest year in the history of the company until Elvis died. The promotion staff broke Hall & Oats, Vickie Sue Robinson, Dr. Buzzards Savannah Band, and Wanted! The Outlaws.

I took the job and began a journey that took me to Harry Nilsson, Chet Atkins, Les Paul, David Bowie, Lou Reed, Waylon Jennings, Guy Clark, Grace Slick, quadraphonic records, Porky & Bess with Ray Charles, Classical music and trips to Nashville, San Francisco, Chicago and Atlanta. Eventually RCA would expand the NY branch and I'd have an office to myself on luxurious Fifth Avenue at 44th Street overlooking the beautiful street clock that Seth Thomas built in 1907.

I had high hopes RCA would be my home for a long time.

Chapter 9
"What's A Guy Like You?"

I got the official letter of employment from RCA Records on October 28, 1975. I'd be reporting to Worthy Patterson and my starting salary would be twice what I made at WB. This offer is contingent upon your passing a pre-employment physical.

I was now working in the RCA home headquarters. This was the place where all the executives executed the plans. I was welcomed in the recording studios, the A&R offices, the product manager offices and like WB, I'd go over to the sales meeting to get beat up once a week about airplay in the market. Elvis was still alive and making records. (I'd work his last record before he passed away.) The building was at 1133 Sixth Ave, at 44th Street. It was a quick two blocks to Bryant Park and the famous Public Library on Fifth Ave. A great place to relax and kick your shoes off on a sunny day between seedy Times Square and elegant Fifth Avenue at 42nd Street.

The actual building was a tall steel structure like so many others on Sixth Ave. Previously I had been working out of a cool townhouse on 50th Street and now I'm in an office building with security cameras and bathrooms miles away. It was intimidating.

The first day I was there I met an A&R guy who introduced me to Lou Reed. Lou and the guy were excited to see a guy like me take over the airplay for them in New York. I'll never forget it when Lou said, "What's a guy like you doing in a place like this?"

Worthy immediately went into action and fashioned an unused conference room into an artist hangout. It had a sofa, a bar and an incredible sound system. A huge plastic RCA Nipper dog was standing watch. At the end of that first day I went upstairs to see Worthy who introduced me to David Cassidy who said, "What's a guy like you doing in a place like this?"

It was a great time to start at the label. It was already on fire. Over at WABC, RCA held the coveted #1 and #2 positions with "Fly Robin Fly" by Silver Convention and "Feelings" by Morris Albert. RCA also had "Miracles" by the Jefferson Starship at #10. My last WB single was "Who Loves You" by the Four Seasons which was now in the Top 5.

I was feeling welcomed and part of the team.

Chapter 10
WNEW FM – The Winds Have Shifted In Our Favor

WNEW FM had a new music director in place as the New Year got started so I invited the guy over to my office and into the promotional records room. It was here he grabbed a disc that had dust on it. It was by an artist named Guy Clark. I was unfamiliar and hadn't heard of him or this disc before. Guy was a country outlaw from Texas. The album had been released and forgotten before I came on board.

The next thing I knew WNEW FM added it into full time rotation. The other add that week was for "Born to Run" by Bruce Springsteen. We were elated! This was the way to kick off the New Year.

With Guy Clark on the air and an open-minded music director at the rock station, RCA was about to make Outlaw County History!

The album was called "Wanted! The Outlaws" and it was made up of Waylon Jennings, Willie Nelson, Tompall Glaser and Jessi Colter. It was the first Country music album to go

Platinum. The rock stations loved it and the sales exploded. RCA was on fire and selling tons of records!

A short time later I got a note from Worthy's boss. He was the big shot that oversaw everyone. The note read:

The new Bobby Bare single, "Drop Kick Me Jesus (Through the Goalposts of Life)," belongs on WNEW FM with Scott Muni. Now is the time to score with this one."

Bobby was a favorite of mine since I heard him on the country & western radio station while my father was driving the old Hudson Hornet. Bobby's hits included "500 Miles," and "Detroit City."

I went over to the big shot's office to pick up the hot wax and when I listened to it I thought it was going to be a chore to get a rock station to support it. The big boss told me the song was a Christian Football Waltz.

Now remember, WNEW FM was a rock station banging Springsteen, so just because the music director picked Guy Clark doesn't add up to the program director digging this novelty Country song. This order was a challenge. WNEW FM was only adding 3-5 records a week and the competition was fierce.

I called Scott Muni and invited him to dinner with Bobby Bare and me. Bobby flew in for the dinner. He wanted to score in a big way.

We went to a joint called Danny's Hideaway and immediately Bobby and Scott got to some heavy drinking. They had both served time in the armed forces and had war stories to exchange. By the time we stumbled out of the Hideaway, Scott and Bobby were fast friends. Scott added the record the following day.

45 RPM (Recollections Per Minute)

It was good time to be working for the Nipper.

By August, Waylon Jennings delivered a more rock leaning effort covering Marshall Tucker Band's "Can't You See," and Neil Young's "Are You Ready for the Country." I brought the record over to WNEW FM and we scored again. The album topped the Country charts and went Gold with four singles. This time we set up a promotion that went like this:

Part 1. A Gold album will be presented to the account that does the best overall job in selling, promoting, and merchandising the Waylon album. A Gold record will also be awarded to the salesman that works closely with the winning account.

Part 2. "Are You Ready for the Country" in conjunction with WNEW FM. A consumer has the chance to win a 30 day unlimited railroad pass on Amtrak to see the U.S.A. We'll supply "x" amount of dollars for extra expenses such as food. The cost: $275.00 for one month unlimited travel. If the Waylon album doesn't go Gold we'll make a special plaque thanking those involved.

The winds had shifted in RCA's favor. After working rock bands like Deep Purple, Black Sabbath and Procul Harum, it was refreshing to see WNEW FM caress the new outlaw country sound. RCA could also rock hard with artists like David Bowie, Lou Reed and the Jefferson Starship. We also had the King – Elvis Presley.

Chapter 11
"Coney Island Baby" – Lou Reed

Lou Reed turned in the tapes that would be his new album called "Coney Island Baby" to his contact guy in the A&R department at RCA. The guy fell in love with what he heard and with Lou's positive attitude. He wanted my full attention on this disc so he turned me on to the tracks before it was released in January of '76.

He told me he wanted this album to succeed for Lou. He felt New York could be the city to break it. He closed the door to his office, lit a joint and turned it up.

There were all kinds of connections to make the story work for the New York radio stations. For airplay, there was "She's My Best Friend," which was originally recorded by Lou's band, the Velvet Underground. The connection to Coney Island could be fun. We could do a live broadcast and invite folks to the boardwalk for free games, rides, hot dogs and beer.

With Lou on board to help promote the record and the great vibe of the album, we all felt we had a winner.

The product manager for Lou was a girl named Doree. She was very personable and well known to many of the key radio people in town. She had been a radio promotion professional and was moving up the ladder to a corporate marketing job.

She came up with an idea to have a party at the Carnegie Hall Cinema. It was in mid-town Manhattan and had a great underground atmosphere. Her thought was to turn this small space on the 7th Avenue entrance to Carnegie Hall into a Coney Island themed party.

A party at the real Coney Island had too many drawbacks. It was now winter in New York City and nobody would want to go to Brooklyn in the evening on a work night.

Doree rented hot dog and popcorn machines and decorated the walls with old amusement park posters. The invitations went out to sales, press and promotion. Lou's album was the big priority at all the sales meetings. Everyone was told to break Lou Reed.

I brought the album around to the rock stations and they were favorably warm to Lou's new effort. The A&R guy got Lou to say yes to radio station visits, so it was time to set things up.

I rented a limo and told the A&R guy to meet me down on the street with Lou. We all jumped in and off we went. Before we hit our first red light, Lou paused and then said to me, "Do you know Doree, my marketing manager?" I said yes.

He said, "I'd like to take her and rip her apart, then put her in a meat grinder and eat her raw."

He then laid into the whole Coney Island Baby event she had set up. He thought it was stupid.

45 RPM (Recollections Per Minute)

"I'm not going to it!" he said.

What could I say? I wasn't his manager or his company A&R guy or his friend, so I backed off. I brushed it aside, and after a few moments of dead silence, I told him how it was going to be when we arrived at WNEW FM. The station folks were excited he was coming and Scott Muni was going to world premier the new album on his show.

Once Lou got on the air he was a sweetheart and happy. Millions of people were hearing his new album. He thanked Scott, he posed for trade photographs, met with fans outside the building and personally told me how great it was to be hearing his music on the radio again.

We got along fine.

Coney Island Baby was well received and Lou and I would work together again over at Arista Records.

Coney Island Baby reached #41 on the charts. It would be his highest charting album until 1989.

Chapter 12
John Denver

I met John at an RCA convention in Chicago. He was kind and sincere and wanted to let me know he'd do anything that made sense when it came to promoting his record. He said we could give away autographed albums and front row seats. He sure didn't need any help from me, but it made me feel good. John and I smoked some grass and had a wonderful talk. I was new and John was a superstar, but we hit it off. He was coming off his smash album, "Windsong," and was shortly going to release "Spirit," his eleventh studio album. I was surprised when I received a personal note from John a few days later.

It was dated March 8, 1976 and John typed it himself. He wrote:

Dear Dave,

I really enjoyed having the opportunity of speaking with you last month and to be able to tell you how much I appreciate your support. I only take this opportunity to reiterate because I want you to know how very important it is to me and how much I think it has to do with what we are doing out there in this world with this music.

The energy that you put into your work, the energy that you give and lend to my music, is totally responsible for the number of people that we are reaching through it. I don't know how to say thank you enough. I would only like you to know that I am pleased to be able to serve this beautiful, magic music and to be able to do so with people like you.

Thank you very much, Peace, John (Denver)

I was moved to receive such a warm and personal letter from John. He was a superstar with much on his mind. He'd even go on to star in motion pictures like, "Oh, God!" with George Burns.

John's tour was coming east and I noticed there was a date in New Jersey. I contacted management and got two front row tickets for my sister-in-law. Backstage after the show, I told John I had some family that would like to meet him and he said, "Of course, do they smoke pot?" I told him no and he said lets fire this up in the bathroom and then bring them back in 10 minutes. The picture of them standing together is a classic. One stoned hippy and two wonderful straight fans.

James Burton was the guitar player in John's band. I knew of James' work and I sought him out. He was incredible. He played with Ricky Nelson's band on the Ozzie & Harriet Show and played all the great licks on "Hello Mary Lou," "Travelin' Man" and was the standout on Dale Hawkins' "Susie Q." These were records I adored. Here it was 1976 and he was still playing with Elvis when he wasn't on the road with John. He was one of the few people I ever asked if we could take a picture together. He was delightful.

Chapter 13
"Station To Station" – David Bowie

I first heard of David Bowie with his very original track called "Space Oddity." The rock stations played it over and over. It actually came out a month before Woodstock and a few days before the Apollo mission to land a man on the Moon. The timing and sound of the record was perfect, however, it wasn't a hit single. Wherever I went, I looked in every store to find a copy, but came up empty. The single and album were hard to find.

In September of '72, Bowie was set to play his first show in New York City at the prestigious Carnegie Hall. I had to get a ticket.

You could feel the energy when the lights went out and Beethoven's 9th Symphony began to play from the soundtrack recording of "Clockwork Orange," and then David hit the stage in bright red hair. It was a true blockbuster introduction. We went wild.

I never imagined one day I'd get to meet him and work with him.

When I arrived at RCA in 1975, the company was putting out "Golden Years" from a new album called "Station To Station." It was a smash. It wound up on WABC and in one week it took a huge jump from #38 to # 13! The single was the follow up to "Fame," David's second biggest hit ever.

A new tour to support "Station To Station" was now underway. The show, set for the 23rd of March, was recorded and played all over the country. To kick off the tour, RCA put out Bowie's "Station To Station" as a single. It was Bowie's longest track ever, running over 10 minutes. The edited single didn't click at Top 40 radio.

Worthy was my boss and we had worked together before so I knew how he operated. He never sent notes or memos, but with Bowie he got pissed at the lack of interest from the staff. A note arrived to everyone that said:

"ONE question was asked on Friday March 5th. What do you think should be the next Bowie single? Attached are the answers received. I do not believe that no one responded."

All he wanted everyone to do was get feedback from the rock stations about which song they may support from the album. Most people could only dream they might have a say in the choice for a David Bowie single.

Finally the radio feedback revealed "TVC 15" should be the next single.

Although none of us knew it at the time, "TVC 15" was about Iggy Pop's hallucination that Bowie's television set had swallowed his girlfriend. Hardly a subject for a Top 40 hit. It failed to reach the Top 50 singles at the time.

"Stay" was the next single, but also failed to win over any Top 40 radio programmers.

Following the show at Carnegie Hall in 1972, Bowie came back and played at Radio City Music Hall on Valentine's Day in 1973. It was a stunner! Bowie opened the show 50 feet above the stage in a cage singing "Hang On to Yourself." It was brilliant.

Finally! It was time to meet the man who fell to earth, the thin white duke, an idol and an icon for me. I was told RCA was having a party for Bowie after his show and I was to invite all the key radio and music trade people.

It was March 26, 1976 and the tour frenzy had built for David's first ever appearance at the huge Madison Square Garden in New York City. The set list was amazing that evening and Bowie was on fire.

After the show, RCA threw a party at the Penn Plaza Club and everyone who was a scene maker turned up. Bowie was sitting with Iggy Pop and Ronnie Spector and I was told to line up the DJ's and bring them over to meet David.

When we were introduced, I told him how great the show was and he told me it was the best reaction he ever received. I told him who I was and what I did and he immediately thanked me for bringing the radio folks to him so he could personally thank them.

Bowie didn't get up as I introduced him. He stayed seated and put out his hand while a photographer did the best he could do to capture the moments. One key radio guy told

Bowie his son went to school with David's kid and they knew each other. David loved that.

After all was said and done, Bowie and his entourage got up to leave. There were tons of people in the room and all of them wanted to meet him, but it was impossible.

As his group was leaving the party he paused and came over to me to say thank you in a most generous way. He reached out and held my hand. I was startled and very moved.

RCA was so interesting at the time. They had everyone from the Kinks to Elvis to Dolly Parton to John Denver. You could not be bored!

Chapter 14
Jefferson Starship – Central Park

In March, on behalf of the Jefferson Starship, RCA gave Scott Muni and WNEW FM a Platinum award for "Red Octopus." It had been a #1 album and had the huge hit "Miracles." Bill Thompson, the Jefferson Starship manager, flew into New York and came with us for the presentation over on Fifth Avenue where WNEW FM was located. Bill had been with the Jefferson Airplane and was a big part of the San Francisco scene. He was the man to know if you were heading out west. Scott loved the attention, and while we were talking, we began a dialog about bringing the band back to Central Park for a free show in July.

In June, RCA released their new disc "Spitfire" and the single "With Your Love." It was a Top 3 albums and getting heavy airplay in the city. Working with WNEW FM, the band and their management, and the city of New York, we were able to have the Jefferson Starship play to 100,000 people in Central Park and have the station broadcast the performance.

A funny thing happened during this time. There was a DJ named Dean Hallam and he was just starting out. He had a part time job selling cut out record albums and he also had a radio show in Connecticut where he called himself Keith McShane and he played rock records. I took him to meet the band backstage.

We ran into Marty Balin, a founding member, who was always quiet and shy and never did interviews. I was always taking Paul Kantner to interviews. He seemed to be the spokesman. When Dean met Marty, he told him he had a ton of Marty's solo album called "Bodacious" which was now a 75-cent cut out. Marty wanted to buy 100 of them on the spot with cash. Dean said he'd bring them to the next show if Marty would do a rare on-air interview with him on his Keith McShane show and autograph five copies of the album to give away. Marty quickly agreed and told Dean to bring the discs to the band's next show.

At the next show, Dean had four big boxes of sealed "Bodacious" albums for Marty and five extras for him to autograph. As this was going down, Paul Kantner walked by with a cigarette hanging from his mouth and said. "Where'd ya get that piece of shit? What a stiff!"

Before I could turn around and see what was going on, Dean shot a stern look at Paul and said, "Hey you, I have ton's more of your stiff solo album lying around the warehouse I can't get rid of, so be quiet!"

I thought Paul was going to punch Dean but he shot back, "Hey man, I'll buy them, too!" And he did! He told Dean/Keith to bring them to the next show. Before 'ya knew it Dean/Keith was a welcome sight backstage at all the Starship shows!

Chapter 15
Hall & Oates

Hall & Oates were two guys from Philly that were signed to Atlantic Records. They were easy going, down to earth guys. Whenever Atlantic had a party for one of their acts, you could be sure the guys were in attendance. They weren't like standoffish rock stars. They went out of their way to meet the DJ's, the salesman, and the Atlantic staff. To make matters even better, they had an incredible song called "She's Gone" that was getting heavy FM airplay. Unfortunately, Atlantic couldn't break the song at Top 40. It looked like the world wasn't going to get a chance to hear "She's Gone."

They finally left Atlantic for greener pastures at RCA records.

In '75, Hall & Oates released what we called "the silver album." The cover was metallic silver and the group used the graphic designer that was responsible for designing David Bowie's "Honky Dory" album cover. The first single from the album stiffed and then something special happened. A radio guy in Cleveland fell in love with the song "Sara Smile," and the phones began to light up from people wanting to hear the song again and again. RCA got in gear and officially released it in January of '76. RCA had to ramp it up so fast we used the product manager's girlfriend for the ad campaign.

By June of '76, "Sara Smile" turned out to be Hall & Oates first Top 10 single.

With a huge hit on their hands, we were not surprised when Atlantic Records re-released "She's Gone" and it exploded, too. It made it into the Top 10 in October of '76.

Their next album, "Bigger Than Both of Us," gave the group their first #1 song called "Rich Girl."

Hall & Oates went on to become one of the most successful recording duos in history.

Years and years later, I'd get a call from their manager who asked me to come onboard as VP of Promotion for a new record label Hall & Oates created.

Chapter 16
The Big Bonus Bucks

It was the time of year for the boss to give you a review. He didn't call you in to his office, he just had paperwork to fill out. Like when we were in school, this was a report card of your progress. If you did well, you were rewarded. Of course, nobody got 100%, since there was always room for improvement. At WB, the most money they ever gave me above my salary was $80.00. I ended up handing it to a tow truck driver who helped me get my car started on a very cold winter Christmas Eve.

I was happy with my salary at RCA and I was really living off my expense account. It paid for my car, phone, restaurants and what seemed like everything except rent and clothing. Since there was no dress code in the music business, I wore jeans and the current free rock group T-Shirt we were giving away.

They paid me well and treated me great.

And so far, I was working well with David Bowie, Lou Reed, David Cassidy, John Denver, Harry Nilsson, Waylon Jennings, Dolly Parton, Charlie Pride and others. They couldn't complain about how I handled myself, and how I always put the artist first and foremost.

At radio, we were getting records on early! Or, at least, on time! Everyone was getting big jumps and great results with our Top 40 songs. We broke Outlaws, Hall & Oats, Dr Buzzards Original Savannah Band and Vickie Sue Robinson. It was RCA's biggest year until Elvis died.

I did notice that the guy in charge of my report card was a guy who didn't go to radio stations with me and wasn't at most of the shows to see what I was doing. I was curious what he thought of my work. It was time to find out.

By year's end, the 1976 RCA Records promotion incentive compensation plans were revealed. This was the special award rating system.

Radio Airplay:

1. What is the timeliness of RCA Records product getting on the air within this market as opposed to other markets?

2. Is RCA Records product getting timely airplay on stations in these markets that are considered to be "breaking" or "reporting" stations?

3. Is RCA Records getting its proportionate share of airplay in this market in relation to the product of competitive record companies?

Artist Relations:

1. Was the home office or artist's manager given advance notice and approval of a planned itinerary for the artists' visit to this market?

2. Was the artists' available time fully utilized while in market?

45 RPM (Recollections Per Minute)

3. When the artist left the market did he feel the visit was beneficial to his career advancement?

Communications with Sales Activities:
1. Is the promotion person always aware of current sales statistics by specific product within his market and nationally?
2. Are the sales people in the market always aware in advance as to all promotions and priority records?
3. Is there coordination between promotion and sales for radio station store reports?
4. Does the promotion person relate well to accounts that report in to make up 'store reports'?

Total Market Coverage:
1. Does the promotion person respond well to specific national R&B direction?
2. Does the promotion person respond well to specific national Country & Western?
3. Does the promotion person respond well to national direction in Jazz & Blues?
4. Are Middle-of-the-Road stations in the market serviced and reported?
5. Are album-programming stations in the market serviced and reported?

General Administration:
1. Are business expense reports done correctly and submitted on a timely basis?
2. Are business expenses in line with budget?

3. Is the weekly tracking report for the market complete?
4. Does the promotion person respond to requests for special reports or follow through on specific instructions?

Worthy's boss sent me his critique the following week. Now, keep in mind, this guy never came to a radio station with me and he never showed up when we brought artists for interviews. On top of that, he never called me. He was a ghost.

He wrote that I wasn't getting records played early in the market and I wasn't always timely with "breaking" artists. He said I should be doing more to get our proportionate share of RCA records on the air as compared to the competitive product.

I was stunned. I was pissed off. I felt like I was a kid back in school getting punished. I realized how wrong he was and yet how much he wanted me to work for him. I thought for a moment. Would I be treated like this at every record company? We were winning and breaking acts and selling tons of records. This shit broke my heart. Every hot shot I worked for at the upper echelon for the rest of my career would all be what I called rumpdogs that you could smell a mile away.

On Total Market Coverage, he wrote that I was less than good to responding well in the R&B direction. Considering Worthy was my boss and mentor and black, this was appalling and way out of line. I'd only been there a few months and RCA had NOTHING at the R&B label for the promotion men to work.

This jerk finished me off by writing, "David, there will not be an any awards at this time. In the future, your contact

45 RPM (Recollections Per Minute)

and handling of the total New York scene will determine awards. Work on it! Timing in New York City will get you call letters WABC."

With Artist Relations he wrote, "Treating them and their managers with sugar will help your relationships. On Sales he wrote, "Get to know your accounts better."

For the rest of my time at RCA he'd always say to me, "Don't stop taking advice. It's one of your strengths."

These so called hot dogs were making hundreds of thousands of dollars off the promotion men, who were responsible for breaking records, and the really big shots were raking in millions more. None of these jerks ever played music for fun. These idiots couldn't even spell Nilsson's name correctly.

But then there were the perks.

Chapter 17
Nashville

The great Cousin Brucie aka Bruce Morrow was a hero of mine. I grew up listening to him spin all the hit records on WABC. He was even on stage when the Beatles played at Shea Stadium in 1965 and 1966. Bruce was the type of guy who couldn't wait to get up every day and meet people. By this time in his career, he did music features for NBC television. I set up interviews for him with Seals & Crofts, Commander Cody & the Lost Planet Airmen, Felix Cavaliere (ex-Rascals) and more.

Bruce called and told me he was headed to Nashville's Music Row for a five day NBC television special and asked me what RCA artists I could deliver. Bruce and his NBC crew were going to be filming at The Exit Inn, Tootsie's Orchid Lounge and Ernest Tubbs Record Shop. Bruce told me he was booking other artists and said I could tag along, too.

We arrived in Nashville and Bruce had it set up to go to Loretta Lynn's home. We'd see her tour bus and get to go horseback riding. She dazzled us when she appeared in a dark blue/purple gown. While Bruce started his interview with

Loretta, I headed out back. The guys that ran her farm asked me if I'd like to go riding, so I jumped on a horse and took off. Her farm seemed bigger than the city of Manhattan, but with no people. It was heaven on earth.

The following day, we went over to Porter Wagoner's studio. Porter loved to wear Nudie suits on stage. Nudie was a celebrity clothing and car designer and one of his early designs for Porter was a peach-colored suit featuring rhinestones, a covered wagon on the back, and wagon wheels on the legs. I was surprised to see him wearing the suit so early in the morning.

Porter had just finished recording a duet with Dolly Parton called, "Say Forever You'll Be Mine." I've since heard Porter had it in the can from a few years earlier. He played it for Cousin Brucie, while the NBC team showed Porter working the soundboard in his studio.

We flipped for the song and thought it was a smash. It became the title of the album by Porter and Dolly Parton.

Nashville was wonderful and working at RCA enabled me to join the Country Music Association and take part in the festivities. I remember one time Worthy asked me to fly down to Nashville for the weekend to meet and hang out with some RCA artists and executives. This was very good news since one of my all time favorite guitar players, Chet Atkins, was an RCA executive running things down in Nashville. That weekend we got to hang out and see Johnny Cash, Marty Robbins, Skeeter Davis and Stonewall Jackson. All of them were legends of the Grand Ole Opry.

A few months later, Dolly Parton released a solo album on RCA and I had the wonderful opportunity to take her around to promote it. It was called, "We Used To."

45 RPM (Recollections Per Minute)

I met up with Dolly earlier in the day and took her to her first radio interview in New York City. It was on WHN, the Country music station. She was smart, sassy, funny, friendly and her smile would light up the room. We talked about Nashville and how nice it is and how everyone knows everyone and they all see each other in the supermarket. Nashville was a town. New York was a city with massive problems that were so big the President was about to address the issue. It was a hot button topic of the moment!

Rather than being interviewed, the programmer allowed her to be the DJ!

It went like this:

"Hi, this is Dolly Parton. I just stopped by to be your hillbilly disc jockey for the day. I thought one thing you needed in New York was a hillbilly and I guess you would call me that."

"You know, I'd like to think that I could do a little better at singing then I do at commercials, and I'd like to do a song now that's been one of my favorite songs that I've written and recorded. It's a song I'd like to thank you for. It kinda compares life to a bargain store and on this day and time, especially in the winter, and especially here in New York, we could all use a bargain and this song is called "The Bargain."

("The Bargain" plays.)

"As I mentioned about a bargain in New York City. I sure hope the President comes through tonight on the news conference 'cause I'm sure you need it and I'm all for you and I'm here to be in the parade tomorrow. I hope you'll all watch me. Now lets hear a commercial from the He-Man shop in Sheepshead Bay."

(Commercial plays and then back to Dolly.)

"They said you could call in so we had many calls from the Bronx and Weehawken and asked for a song that I'm glad you like. It started a streak of hit records for me. It's called, "Jolene."

("Jolene" plays.)

"This is the latest record I have out. I write a lot of songs and some of them are sad and some are just plum pitiful and that's what this one is. It's called, "We Used To."

("We Used To" plays.)

"Well that's Dolly Parton and so am I. I wanna take just a minute now and say thanks to all the people that are listening and also the folks here at the station helping to make it possible for me to be nominated and voted on the #1 Female Vocalist of the Year. I'm a smart person, smart enough to know that there are many deserving people with more talent than me, but I want you to know you couldn't have given it to anybody that was any more proud of it than me. Thank you.

"As we mentioned a while ago, people are calling in and we had a lot of requests for "The Coat of Many Colors," and this song means more to me then all the other songs I've ever written and recorded because it's a true story of my childhood and it happened when I was 8 years old around this time of year and all of the words are true."

("Coat of Many Colors" plays.)

"Here's a song I sung with a man that has helped me very, very much in my career. A man I'll always love and respect. I hope this is a favorite of yours. Here's Porter Wagoner and myself singing "If Teardrops Were Pennies."

("If Teardrops Were Pennies" plays.)

Dolly ended her disc jockey stint with the following:

45 RPM (Recollections Per Minute)

"President Ford will be holding a news conference tonight and unless 'aid' is like a butterfly, New York might be getting some."

The following morning I met Dolly and handed her the New York Daily News where the headline read:

"FORD TO CITY - DROP DEAD" – Vows He'll Veto Any Bailout.

Dolly laughed out loud and screamed, "SHIT!"

Chapter 18
Elvis Presley

Elvis was the King of Rock & Roll. I first saw him on the cover of a record called "50,000,000 Fans Can't Be Wrong." It came out in 1959 and showed the King wearing a bow tie and a gold-lame suit with a curl of his hair wildly hanging down on his face. It was a bold statement and got my attention. I was six years old and playing hide and seek at my cousin's home when I found myself ducking underneath the big radio console and seeing it for the first time. I picked it up to look at it and my cousin told me to put it down since it was his brother's album. Turns out they weren't allowed to play it. It was sad for me to watch that record lay there for years collecting dust. I can say for sure that although my cousin had that record, he sure never played it. I'd have to wait a long time to hear what 50,000,000 fans already knew.

Up at RCA I had only one question since the day I arrived. How do we get to meet the King? I asked my boss if he ever met the King and he said no. I asked the folks in the A&R department and they all said they never met him. They said he never comes to New York City to the home office.

The King was touring in 1976, so I asked if I could go to a show on the road and meet him. The closest he got was Rochester and Syracuse in late July. I asked around and nobody could hook up a meeting. It seemed that nobody at RCA knew the King and nobody cared about going to see him.

The only time I got to see Elvis in concert was at Madison Square Garden back in '72. It was Elvis' first complete show ever in New York City. Previously, he had only performed on television shows in New York. A friend of mine, who was younger than me and wasn't even born when "Hound Dog" came out, stood on line for days to get better seats than the celebrities sat in. Elvis apparently wanted only fans to be close to him while he was performing. We actually sat in front of a few guys from Led Zeppelin and a few members of the Rascals.

Then Worthy called and said, "Morrell, we're heading to Memphis. Pack your bags. Colonel Tom Parker called the home office and invited a few head honchos to see a show and meet Elvis on July 5."

I threw my fist in the air and shouted, "Fantastic!"

It was late June and I had a week to get ready. Elvis was from Memphis so this was going to be extra special plus it was the United States Bicentennial on July 4, 1976 and everyone all over the great nation would be celebrating that evening. In New York City they were gathering the greatest array of tall ships anywhere in the world to sail on the Hudson River.

I took a suitcase out of the basement and began packing for the greatest day since I met John Lennon. I had met so many artists on my journey, but Elvis was the true King and I couldn't wait to shake his hand. I was thinking, should I wear

45 RPM (Recollections Per Minute)

a pair of blue suede shoes? Should I wear a 50's leather jacket? Should I push my hair back? Should I bring color and black & white film? The questions were endless. I was all goosed up!

We were now three days out from our flight and I was counting the hours.

"Moody Blue" was the final studio album from Elvis. It included four tracks from his final recording session in October of 1976. The album also featured some live recording that ended up being the final recordings he ever made. The single, "Moody Blue," was released in late November of '76 and went to #1 on the Country charts, the last #1 of his lifetime.

I brought the album up to WNEW-FM but got the door shut. I told everyone at the station that was on the air to just mention that Elvis had a new album and drop the needle on a track and let people hear what Elvis was recording.

Nobody wanted to give the rock audience a taste of what Elvis was up to. I even went to the ol' General of the station, Scott Muni, but he said no. I thought that was the end of it, but then a year later Elvis died. I put on WNEW-FM that fateful afternoon in August of '77.

It was unbelievable to hear Scott crying over Elvis' death on the air and then treating the audience to the King's last work. I was boiling, listening to him talk so highly about a record he said he wouldn't play.

It was his last album to reach the Top 40 before he passed. To mark the occasion of "Moody Blue," RCA pressed it in blue vinyl.

Meanwhile, it was time to hit the hay and think about meeting the King in Memphis!

Chapter 19
The Rumpdogs Are On The Phone

I was toweling off my wet hair and groovin' to Stevie Wonder late one morning when the phone rang. It was an operator telling me to get ready for an emergency RCA conference call with the head man. I couldn't have imagined what it was about. The only thing on my mind was leaving town and heading to Memphis to meet the King.

In moments the call started.

It was an RCA blowhard that nobody liked. Here's what he said to us:

"Many of you have heard and know what's happened. I want to speak directly to you so you'll understand. Worthy Patterson is leaving the company."

Worthy was the guy who brought me to RCA. He was the guy who took me from the warehouse to become a promotion man. Worthy was my main man. This was a serious blow to me.

The head honcho went on.

"There are a couple of things you should know that are important. We haven't been doing too well in the charts lately and we shouldn't let ourselves get depressed."

He was full of shit and now I began to steam up.

"We've got a lot of good records out there and at this point we came up with the best third quarter in history and it looks like we'll have the best year in our history."

That's right! And, it's because of Worthy and his promotion team!

"I want to insure you people there is no intention of any kind of mass changes. You people represent a fine promotional force and have nothing to be ashamed about."

Ashamed? Who the fuck was he talking to? I burped the word 'asshole' into the phone so he'd hear it.

"At this point we have no replacement for Worthy. We are counting on you being professionals and we're counting on continuing to move some records and not lose any steps.

"Promotion will be reporting to Marketing. I know you've heard tons of rumors, but everything is behind us now. We've had problems, now their gone. We have to focus and bring some records home. I know it won't be easy. All we wanna do is get records played and sell them. I think we have enough things out there and enough potential. We have a lot of fine records out there."

This rumpdog was losing grip and beginning to stutter. He was a nervous wreck and I, for one, wanted to give him a black eye.

"What you did with Hall & Oates, Vicky Sue Robinson, Dr. Buzzards Savannah Band, you have to follow up. It means a lot of money for all of us."

45 RPM (Recollections Per Minute)

This crack reminded me of the Mothers of Invention album, "We're Only In It For The Money."

"John Travolta is a good record for your Pop stations. Pittsburgh and Miami are getting calls. The new Pure Prairie League is a different sound for them and is a good rock & roll record, it's the title of the album. I think we're in the ballgame with that record. The Whispers is a new record we hope to go Top 10. On the group Chocolate Milk, we have a good black spread, and a new Soul Train Gang pulling in some early stations.

"That's the core as we see it now. New records include L.A. Jets, a complete departure from their first album. Dave & Sugar's "Rumbling" is doing well at Country, along with Dickey Lee. Ray Charles' "Oh Lord, I'm On My Way" needs help, too.

"We're tying to push those singles that are tied into albums and are long term artists for us. If we can break any single, we're talking about another million units. If anyone on this call has any kind of problems or concerns, or any doubts, call us. We have to get a momentum going."

I wanted to fart into the phone.

Meeting Elvis wasn't happening anymore. The trip to Memphis would be cancelled.

Eventually, when I caught up to Worthy, he told me what happened. He said RCA was pouring tons of promotional money into independent promotion support and he felt RCA didn't need the extra help. Worthy said he'd rather give the money to his team for the job they did. The rumpdogs however, were swamped with nasty calls from the tip sheet publishers, independent promotion companies, product managers and artists wanting this additional support.

The rumpdogs won out.

Slowly but surely, Worthy's staff left RCA, but not before the rumpdogs found out life's lesson that Stevie Wonder sang about:

"Just because a record has a groove, don't make it in the grove."

Chapter 20
20th Century Fox Records

I got a call asking me if I'd be interested in joining 20th Century Fox Records. It would be my first regional job and I'd get to travel all over the East Coast. The good news was the office location. I'd be high in the sky with an office on the 42nd floor in Midtown Manhattan. Even better was the delight I felt when I found out ex-Capitol Records president Alan Livingston was running the joint.

When I met Mr. Livingston, I presumed everyone else at 20th would know his background as well I did. Alan Livingston was something cool! He created Bozo the Clown. He was there for the Beatles phenomenon. His wife was a movie star! She starred in one of the all time greatest films, "Sunset Boulevard." She was with him when he heard "I Want to Hold Your Hand" for the very first time and she didn't like it.

I chewed his ear off for as long as he could take it and he liked me. I got into a long conversation with him in my office about the Beatles' "Yesterday & Today" album. This was the famous incident where the Beatles posed as bloody butchers with meat and dolls for their album cover. It was deemed tasteless and Capitol, under Livingston's command, withdrew the cover from the market. Tons of Beatles albums had to be returned and a new image was pasted over the old one. It became one of the most sought after album covers of all time. I owned John Lennon's personal copy and wanted to go deep with Livingston on the subject.

He enjoyed every moment of our conversation but I had no idea to what extent he'd take my interest. We shook hands and he told me he was in town to look at some footage of a film he thought was going to be huge. It was called "Star Wars," and he told me I'd be working it. We said goodbye and off he went.

Then, a few weeks later, something wonderful happened. The mailman delivered a package to my desk.

I opened the package and an album was inside with a note that read:

Dear David, I hope you'll find room for this in your Beatle collection. Alan.

I put the note aside and there in front of me was an original 1966 sealed Beatle Butcher cover from the collection of the ex-president of Capitol Records.

I almost fainted!

We'd become so close he actually went home and looked in his closet and sent me a copy.

Under Alan's command, 20th Century went on to have a few hits. Some of them you may not remember. Kenny Nolan's, "I Like Dreamin'," spent over 20 weeks on the chart and ended up in the Top 5, Peter McCann's, "Do You Wanna Make Love," which went Top 5 and Dan Hill's, "Sometimes When We Touch," which made it to the Top 3!

45 RPM (Recollections Per Minute)

Every one of these guys was terrific. Kenny Nolan gave me a Gold disc that I hung at my mother's house. Peter McCann gave me an expensive leather wallet with a rare Indian head nickel in it for good luck and Dan Hill, besides handing me his wallet, socks and shoes before going on stage each evening, gave me a story for the ages I'll share with you in the upcoming Carly Simon chapter.

For Alan Livingston, 20th Century Fox had budgeted a million dollars a year for three years to support the revived label, and it began paying its own way after only six months.

On the album side, we had a few corkers that were destined for the cutout bin. Sandy Baron, the comedian, is a perfect example of an album that got zero airplay after people heard it. "All This and World War II" was another one that's impossible to explain. It was World War II footage with Beatles songs, sung by others, playing throughout. The New York Daily News said the film's PG rating stood for "Positively Ghastly!" The lineup on the soundtrack looked good on paper, but nobody supported it and besides, they'd rather play the original Beatle records and not have to mention a movie that was impossible to explain. The disc included performances by Elton John, Rod Stewart, The Bee Gees, The Four Seasons, Peter Gabriel and Tina Turner.

We had a few huge selling Barry White albums and a rock album fronted by Doors keyboardist Ray Manzarek called Nite City. Danny Sugerman, who started working in the Doors office when he was a teenager and became their manager after Jim Morrison died, managed them.

The band came to New York City and we hit the road. It was a tough beginning since we stayed up all night getting loaded in a hotel room overlooking Central Park with dozens of candles lit. The actor-comedian, Sandy Baron, stopped by at some ungodly hour of the morning to get lit up with us. The following day was a Monday and it was raining. We made it to Philadelphia and went to the venue for the soundcheck when we were told there was a transit strike in town. So with a crummy, cold, rainy evening in downtown Philly, with a strike going on, the place was practically empty for the first show. Ray was coming off a bad hangover and gave it his all. He even played an incredible keyboard solo version of the Doors, "Light My Fire."

Nobody was lining up outside for the second show, so Ray asked everyone to stay. All of a sudden I spotted Harrison Ford, Carrie Fisher and Mark Hamill, the three stars of "Star Wars." They were in Philly for promotion and were being escorted by someone I knew from the New York office. Harrison spent his time on the phone renting a Thunderbird to drive home. He didn't want to fly.

After the second show it was late, so we hit a dive bar to chill. It was just Danny, Ray and I. We asked for a drink, but the guy said they were done serving. We headed to the bathroom when a man walked in and asked us what was going on. We told him we just stopped in for a drink, but the bar was closed. All of a sudden he pulls out a gun and points it at the ceiling and fires it. It blew our ears out and scared us to death. He said, "Lets go back out there, I know the bartender." We freaked out, but we also took him up on his drink offer. Nite City is long forgotten, but the evening in Philly has left me without a good left ear.

45 RPM (Recollections Per Minute)

Ambrosia was another band that showed potential, but at this point they were a turntable hit. That's a record that people like to hear but don't go out and buy.

Between my office and the foyer was a small screening room run by an old man who was finishing up his career. He was watching the rushes of a new movie coming out called "Star Wars." None of us knew what the heck the movie was, but it reminded me of when I worked at WB and saw "The Exorcist" and "Blazing Saddles" for the first time in an advance screening, and had no idea what was about to unfold.

History was about to be made with the movie "Star Wars." John Williams created a classical score masterpiece that would cross over to pop radio and even get played on the blockbuster Top 40 station WABC, even ahead of the novelty version by Meco. The old man in the screening room invested his small dollars wisely and had the last laugh.

To promote the soundtrack, I got the studio to send under lock and key a Wookie costume. I promptly called my brother and told him to get ready to take a few days off school. A road trip was in order. I took him to NYC, Long Island and Philadelphia and everywhere we went everyone wanted a photograph. He was so popular in the costume he didn't take the head off no matter how hot it got that summer.

Chapter 21
Carly Simon

It was May 12, 1977 and Carly Simon was booked to perform at the Other End in Greenwich Village. What a night it would be. Carly was shy and rarely performed, which made it even more special.

I had been working with Dan Hill who was having a hit with "Sometimes When We Touch" and he was playing at the club for a few evenings. I went every night and tried to bring as many key people as I could. Dan was the type of guy who performed without shoes and gave you his wallet to hold before going on. He'd look you right in the eyes when he spoke and was very grateful for all the hard work I'd done for him.

On the last evening of Dan's show down at the club, I was hanging out with the owner, Paul Colby. Paul was a songplugger or what we now called a promotion man, and he went on to work for Frank Sinatra and Duke Ellington. I could listen to him speak all night. He told me Carly Simon was coming to play and since he'd seen me work so hard the past few days, he said I could come and he'd give me a table for four right up front. I was thrilled!

At first I thought of bringing the WABC folks. They never saw her live but were supporting her huge hits. Then I thought of inviting the FM gang over at WNEW since they loved her too and played many tracks from all her records. But then I told myself to wait a minute and don't turn this invitation into work. Have fun with it. So I decided for the first time in memory to invite my brother and some friends and turn it into a party. They know how to have a good time and laughter is the best medicine. Besides, I wanted to enjoy myself and not worry about the other person having fun.

Four tickets cost $16 bucks! The booze bill was $91.35. The bill was for 24 beers and 28 tequila shots! You may say we were lit!

Our first call of order was to the waitress who promptly brought us four beers and four tequilas. Yummy! "Miss, we'll have another round over here when you get a moment."

Right before show time my brother went to the bathroom and I tagged along, but when we entered the men's room the only stall available was being used. My brother had to go pronto since he only rented the beer, so he whipped it out and pissed in the sink.

I was shocked, but it was too late. There was nothing I could do but hope no one walked in. While he was peeing in the sink, the person in the stall came out to wash his hands. It was James Taylor and he was headed to the sink to wash his hands, but stopped abruptly when he saw my brother.

45 RPM (Recollections Per Minute)

We just stood there laughing uncontrollably while James totally understood and laughed, too. At this very moment the door swung open and in walks Mick Jagger.

"Awright boys. Who's gonna powder my nose?" he barked.

My brother was still pissing away and wasn't aware of James Taylor and Mick Jagger standing there in bewilderment.

"My hands are full Mick, I'm trying to get my brother out of here." I said.

"Awright girls, come over here," he said as he put the coke spoon into the vile he had in his pocket and put it right up to my nose. I inhaled and felt that rush that could fly me to the moon.

Back at our upfront table, we were singing as loud as we could with the other 200 people in the club. As we were all screaming, "You're so vain, I'll bet you think this song is about you," I was thinking about Mick and wondering if he to was singing at the top of his lungs, too.

Her band of New York session players included David Spinozza, Hugh McCracken, Rick Marotta and Tony Levin. Carly performed over a dozen hits including her recent single, "Nobody Does It Better," and then brought up James Taylor to sing "Close Your Eyes." I felt as though I sitting in the middle of great stereo album taking place live. These were songs she never sang live before and Carly was bringing them to life.

The show was incredible and yet nothing came of it as far as Carly taking this band and going out to tour. This was truly a once in a lifetime event.

The boys and me were so wasted we forgot where we parked and when we finally figured it out our car had been towed. By the time we sobered up and had the car back it was coming on 5am. I didn't have to work the next day but the gang did. When we dropped off one of the guys his wife was in the upstairs window yelling at the top of her lungs, "Where the hell have you been? Don't you know it's 5 o'clock in the morning?" Then she gave me the evil eye, followed by the finger.

I got home and fell in bed laughing. I put on the radio and heard them play James Taylor. I thought of calling the hotline and filling in the DJ to the events of the last twelve hours, but decided to fire up a joint and sleep till noon.

What a night!

Chapter 22
Arista

After meeting with Arista's VP of Promotion, I accepted the job to be in charge of New York City radio promotion. My new boss was a guy who wasn't interested in getting records broken out of New York City. He knew better. He set his sights on spending money with the trade magazines, independent promotion people and stations that had a reputation of breaking records. For New York, he just wanted someone he could rely on to get the hits played on time and not late. He wasn't going to be busting my balls. Believe it or not, this guy had been studying to be a priest in St. Louis before entering the sinful record business. One time he even told me he saw a man throw up a cue ball during some ritual he witnessed!

Now it was time to meet Clive Davis, the president, and let him know Arista had a new man with experience to get records played.

The only thing I knew about Clive was that he was fired from Columbia Records and sued for alleged personal use of company funds. In Walter Yetnikoff's book, "Howling at the Moon," he writes, "Clive was called to the office and canned.

He was served with a civil complaint by CBS for expense account violations and escorted out of the building."

I had been over at Billboard earlier in the week and asked the chart editor about Clive. He took me to a file cabinet and took out a manila envelope with press clippings in it. It had everything I needed to get familiar with the man.

The first thing I saw was a profile piece on Clive that was done when he was 33 years old. What struck me first was how late he was to come into the music business. He had been a lawyer all the way up to this point. Corporate law was his field. The article said Clive was able to observe and participate in such matters as the Federal Trade Commissions record club talks and Columbia's acquisition of the Fender Guitar Company.

I found that Clive wasn't involved at all with finding songs, signing artists or developing anyone's career. At the time Columbia had a predominance of lawyers in its key executive positions. It was unlikely any of these lawyers ever attended marketing, sales and promotion meetings. It was completely unlikely they knew anything about WABC, WNEW FM, the tastemakers running these stations, or how music actually got added to the radio stations.

Unlike me who loved rock and roll, it said Clive's favorite thing to do was go to the theater. I guess he must have loved the Broadway show "Beatlemania," since he released the music from the show as a two record set.

Clive, at the time, was as far away from the creative side as possible. For him it was all law and suits.

There was nothing about him that was interesting. He wasn't finding groups, songs or had anything to do with radio

45 RPM (Recollections Per Minute)

promotion, marketing or sales. Clive was reading legal contracts. The Billboard story said while he was in school he was interested in copyright law and studied it.

A photograph I saw showed him standing with a bunch of suits in front of an Engineering Research and Development Center in Milford, CT. He was there to dedicate a building.

On the other hand, I was 25 years old when I stood in his office for the first time. I already had more than half a decade working hit records in the toughest city with the tightest playlists. I knew how the job got done. My career started in the warehouse picking and packing records, attending sales and promotion meetings. I was going to concerts and meeting promoters, managers and bands. I had experience working with the Allman Bros. Band, James Taylor, Frank Sinatra, Deep Purple, Neil Young and many others.

I looked at my watch. It was nearing 10pm. I wondered why everyone was still in their offices working. I sure wasn't hearing music being played. Clive's office was big with a high ceiling. There was no music playing and it was cold. He stood up and shook my hand.

He asked me sit down and then he started asking me questions about my success working soundtracks over at 20th Century Fox Records. I thought it was strange since I didn't come over here to work those kinds of records. He immediately grilled me on a film score by Georges Delerue, from the movie "Julia." I was dumbfounded but went along with him to see where he was going. He started asking me about the John Williams score to "Star Wars". I told him the movie was a phenomenon and I made sure Rick Sklar from WABC saw an advance screening. Once the movie became a blockbuster,

85

everyone was looking to score points with the franchise. There was even a novelty version of the "Star Wars Cantina Theme" that was climbing the Top 40 charts, but I made sure Rick was aware of the tremendous sales the soundtrack was achieving. When it was time to commit WABC to playing something from "Star Wars," Rick went with the true hit from John Williams.

He kept it up on these film scores 'till I had to look at my watch. A half hour had passed and I felt a yawn coming on.

I was hoping he'd play me some hit music before I left, but that never happened. I asked him about Bob Dylan, but he shooed me off. I wanted to hear what he had coming out on the release schedule, but he wasn't going there.

I liked Marvin Gaye he liked Doris Day. I'd push him on his relationships and he'd push back on soundtracks and scores.

I thought Clive was a music guy, but he came off as a businessman. I thought he was someone who understood and had knowledge of getting records played in New York. I figured he had a relationship with Rick Sklar, the PD of WABC and Scott Muni, the PD of WNEW FM. These two guys were based in New York and were the most influential tastemakers at the time. To get a record played full time on the radio you had to have a thumb up from these men.

If Clive knew these guys, the best I could do was listen to what he had to say. But if Clive didn't know them, I'd have the upper hand.

I learned Clive didn't have a relationship with them.

I asked him some hot questions that needed answers. I asked about his relationship with Scott Muni at WNEW FM, I

45 RPM (Recollections Per Minute)

asked him about Rick Sklar at WABC, but he was ducking and he scoffed as though he was dismissing me.

I realized quickly he didn't have a clue of what it takes to get a record on WABC and WNEW FM. None whatsoever. He never did the job.

It was getting late and his office was so cold you could hang meat in there.

I got up and he shook my hand with the pat on the back routine. I wasn't sure if I was headed for success or the electric chair.

I was happy I stood my ground with Clive and my new boss. Things were bound to get tough and I had to make sure the line in the ground was clearly drawn.

In his book, "Rocking America," Rick Sklar wrote the following about Clive and his behavior. "Clive Davis held a party at his Manhattan apartment....cigarettes, cigar ashes and food were ground into the carpets and drinks spilled on sofas and chairs. I remember my wife asking me who was going to pay for all the damage. Sure enough, the cost of repairs were one of the items cited by Columbia when they decided to part company with Clive."

Clive, in two books, doesn't site Rick at all. I was surprised to see more was said of Jackie Gleason and Gomer Pyle (Jim Nabors) than Rick or tastemaker and program director Scott Muni of WNEW FM, the powerhouse FM rock station.

I left with the notion that I could succeed getting the Arista hits played on radio early or on time without any interference from my boss or Clive.

Chapter 23
"Street Hassle" – Lou Reed

Lou had a new album called "Street Hassle" and we got word he was ready to work it. His manager was a 7-foot bald man and his private chauffeur was 4 feet high with a beat down limo that was falling apart.

The car had a bad inspection sticker and whenever we stopped at a radio station the man put a newspaper under the windshield wiper to hide the view of the sticker in case a policeman was walking by. The license plate was tied on with a rope that the driver had to adjust. The car smelled of gasoline and the seats were torn and ragged. It was a piece of shit that should have been junked years ago.

Lou was a handful so I asked the boss to come along with me. He had zero interest in Lou so he told me to take a guy named Lenny who worked for him. Lenny and I met at the office and headed over to a hotel to meet the manager. This guy was someone we didn't know and had no prior management experience, so he was in the dark, too, as to what was going to happen.

We told him exactly where we were going and what we hoped to accomplish and we hoped Lou would be on his best behavior and talk about his new record and what his plans were to tour behind it. He seemed to understand and said Lou was onboard and there would be no problems.

When we got downstairs we saw a car that looked like it lost a demolition derby. It was a beat up limo all dented. We saw Lou's driver standing there trying to hide the expired inspection sticker posted in the windshield. He was little guy with no teeth he was waiting for us, while fending off the hotel doorman to move the car.

The gang of us pulled up on Christopher Street in front of Lou's joint. The manager said he'd be right out. Forty minutes later the door opens and Lou hops in and says out loud, "Who are these guys?" We chuckled and then Lou turned to his manager and said, "I'm not kidding, who are these two?" After the bullshit stopped and the manager felt bad, the car headed out and things toned down a few notches.

Things went well up at WNEW FM and we headed over to WPIX FM, a station that was open to new music and run by the great programmer George Taylor Morris. Things went really well. The DJ that did the interview was John Oogle who leased Lou's apartment when Lou toured overseas. Because of their relationship the interview was seamless and interesting.

Lou genuinely liked the other staff members so we took some photographs and began to leave. Sitting at the switchboard was a DJ, and as Lou was walking by to leave the guy made a comment. I didn't hear what it was, but Lou screamed at him and all hell broke loose. By the time things settled down again we were in the car heading back to headquarters.

45 RPM (Recollections Per Minute)

Twenty minutes later, Lou breathed a sigh of relief and said, "I think things went well today, thanks fellas. Wanna smoke a joint?" We said "hell yeah" and kicked back to enjoy ourselves.

We arrived back at Arista and Lenny and I got off on the 6th floor while Lou headed to Clive's office. All of a sudden the phone rang and it was Clive asking us to come to his office. As soon as we walked in and the door was closed Clive looked at us and stated, "Lou says both of you were smoking pot in the car today. Is this true?"

Before I could even gulp, Lenny blurted out, "No, Lou is lying!" Lou was sitting there smirking, hoping we'd twist under Clive's scrutiny, but Lenny was ruthless. "We busted our ass for this guy today. No one wanted him, but we twisted arms. Lou's got a bad reputation at radio because he curses on the air and we got the job done! We went on the air, shook hands and took pictures. WNEW FM even wants him back!"

"Okay you're dismissed," Clive said.

We were pissed. Believe it or nuts, an hour goes by and Len and I head out of the office together and guess what? We run into Lou in the elevator. You could feel the tension.

I said, "Hey Lou, out with the bad air, in with the good air."

Lou was pissed off.

Lenny asked him what the outburst was all about. Lou told us to fuck ourselves. When we hit the street we invited Lou to join us at the bar of a restaurant on 56th Street.

Lenny and I were sitting at the bar when the goon limo driver came in and said, "Lou's outside in the car. He wants you guys to come outside and get in the car." Lenny pointed his finger into the guy's chest and pushed him while saying, "We're here. Inside. Tell Lou to come in or go home!" Forty-five minutes went by and that car stayed put with no one getting in or out. Finally the driver came back in and asked us to come to the car one more time. We both told him to go fuck himself.

The car pulled away and that was the last we saw or heard from Lou Reed.

We knew we had a great story to tell others for the rest of our lives but we also knew we wanted nothing to do with getting airplay on "Street Hassle" so we just stopped talking about it to anyone. I went home and pulled my Lou albums, and rather than give them to someone who digs him, I tossed them all in the garbage.

Chapter 24
WABC Radio
The Biggest And Greatest Station Of All Time

The man in charge was Rick Sklar. He ran the powerhouse radio station and nothing got past him. He was corporate. If you were a promotion man and visited the station weekly, you learned and knew what to expect. You learned how to work with Rick if you wanted to succeed and have his respect. Rick was clear and articulate when it came to what he was looking for in a record to succeed and be a hit.

The man behind Rick was Glenn Morgan who started at the station in 1971 and rose to program director in 1975. Together they were Batman & Robin in Gotham City. Winning every battle.

In Rick's book, he writes about the genesis of the giant radio station WABC. He says, "To achieve this control of the dial would require extreme selection on our part. I would have to find universally appealing music that would attract almost everybody. Each record would have to do triple demographic duty, or I could not afford to play it. I wasn't making too many friends. As the playlist got shorter and shorter, tempers at the record companies got hotter and hotter. To generate the biggest ratings in radio, I used the shortest playlist in the business. Most new songs just did not appeal to all the diverse groups that made up our target audience."

Personally, I'd been hearing this mantra since I walked in the door of the music business back in June of '72. I met Rick over the years at many WB parties, and I began to work him on records back in February of '74. I knew a good relationship with Rick was key to my survival as a promotion man in New York City. I knew the rules and never took them for granted. I knew when to take a record to Rick and always got them on the air early or on time, never late.

At Arista, I began to get notes from Clive about records he wanted me to take to WABC. Never did he ask me to come up and listen to the songs. He just wanted them on the air. It was odd to get these notes since the pressure never came from my direct boss and I never got a note from Mo Ostin or Joe Smith, the two Presidents at WB, or any president for that matter. Clive wanted songs on WABC that were not only stiffs in New York, but also national stiffs.

When a company is cold, it's the staff that keeps getting the beating, never the overpriced big shots. With all the money in the world, Arista couldn't find the next hit. Golden ears, my ass.

At the end of Rick's book he has a yearly list of the songs that got the ratings. Besides Barry Manilow, Arista had nothing. Zero. Nada.

45 RPM (Recollections Per Minute)

Even though Arista 45's weren't monster hits, and aren't heard on oldie stations, I did manage to get play on WABC with Al Stewart, Melissa Manchester, the Patti Smith Group, John Williams and Raydio.

Chapter 25
"Because The Night" - Patti Smith Group

Besides the soundtrack to "Close Encounters of the Third Kind," Arista had no records in the Top 50 album chart. You could cut the tension at the office with a knife. The winter cold had left a bitter frost on the Arista releases.

Finally, on March 22, the single I was waiting for came out. It was produced by Jimmy Iovine and written by Bruce Springsteen. It was called, "Because the Night" and was the new rock track from the Patti Smith Group.

I knew Jimmy since John Lennon introduced us back in '74 while Jimmy was working on "Born To Run" and John's "Rock 'n' Roll" album. He was 16 years old at the time.

I knew Lenny Kaye from Patti's band since he was a music writer for a girlie magazine called "Cavalier." Lenny had written a piece on my rare Beatle collection. Lenny was also responsible for putting together the great album of garage music called "Nuggets." A must record for any collection.

Lenny was now in Patti's band and it was great to be working with him.

Ivan Kral, who played bass in Patti's band, was one of my closest friends. We met seven years earlier when Ivan was working for Apple/Abkco. Ivan's girlfriend worked at the Bottom Line club where we all hung out regularly.

Jimmy called me and said to come over to the Record Plant. He was very excited and wanted me to hear his newest masterpiece. He could barely contain himself.

When I got there he told me he thought he found the right radio record for Patti. She had reworked the original demo of a song Bruce Springsteen had written and branded it her own.

He started up the tape machine and threw the volume up. I didn't know what to expect. Patti's music was always an acquired taste but this was melodic, well written and to the point. It was powerful.

When it finished, I looked at Jimmy and told him he had a winner. I told him my mission would be much bigger than just delivering it to the rock stations. I was going to make it my mission to take it to the top! I believed in the song so much I thought I'd begin a campaign to get it played on WABC, the Top 40 station. Nothing could be crazier than to think Patti's music would be heard alongside the top hits of the day.

Of course, we'd have to start it at the rock stations and get the whole staff excited. I mailed personal notes with each record and mentioned Patti would be working the song and we'd be stopping by the radio station.

Patti was ready to whip New York into shape. I called for a limo and headed downtown to pick her up.

45 RPM (Recollections Per Minute)

Patti lived with Allen Lanier from Blue Oyster Cult who owned the place at Fifth Avenue and 8th Street, above the hip restaurant called 1/5 Ave. I told the driver to go tell the doorman we're outside and ready to go. He came back with a message for me.

"She wants you to go upstairs." Shit, we're running late already.

I took the elevator up to her floor and when I got off there was a door ajar and Patti came out with a toothbrush in her mouth and toothpaste running down her face. It was quite a site.

She invited me in and told me hang out for a few minutes. She was almost ready. The apartment was very large and white and empty of any furniture. I didn't know if she was moving in or out. I walked to the windows and looked down on Fifth Avenue with a view of Washington Square Park.

I went to the sink and poured myself a glass of water.

Patti came back out of a bedroom and said, "Come on in."

I walked into a bedroom of disarray. Clothes and books were everywhere. She was sitting on the bed and introduced me to her assistant, Andi.

All of a sudden the emptiness I felt in the other room was gone and we were cuddled up comfortable while Patti was getting ready. She was a pro, a circus trainer and a lion tamer. She put on her Bowler hat and was ready to rule the New York City airwaves. It was a powerful image to behold.

I took Patti up to the progressive 'punk' station, WPIX FM, where new wave music was being heard full time. The music director was a gal named Meg Griffin who went on to

Dave Morrell

make quite a name in the music business. I met her upstate in Westchester, NY, where she was working with a new guy named Howard Stern. Howard had short hair and wore Izod short sleeve shirts in those days. We'd go out on the back highways listening to rare Beatle tapes. Howard loved it. He loved the Beatles too.

At WPIX FM, John Oogle and Dan Neer did a show they called Radio Radio and that's the place we wanted Patti to be the featured interview. Besides her new album, "Easter," she also brought her book, "Babel," to talk about. It was a book of her poems and prose.

John Oogle did the interview and was extraordinary. He was the go-to guy if you had to bring an artist up to the radio station. When I brought Patti, they remembered going to college together and being in plays together. Patti glowed and the interview was great.

Things were going great with Patti until we went up to WNEW FM.

The night I took her up to WNEW things got crazy. She wasn't comfortable with the late night guy doing the interview and wasn't clear if he was on her side. She told me to tell him not to play a song by a band with a member she had a relationship with, so I called him and told him not to play anything by him on the night we come up. Sure enough, while driving to the station at midnight, the DJ plays the taboo band. Patti goes from being light and fun to full time nuts. Everything ran off the rails. She cursed him and screamed, but with all the buildup, she couldn't tell him to go fuck himself. She was a pro and went full speed ahead.

45 RPM (Recollections Per Minute)

The interview, which should have been fun and celebratory, was over quickly.

After dropping Patti off at 2am, I headed home to get some sleep, but my phone rang at 3am. It was the DJ who was now how crying in his soup. It was pathetic.

I had to forge ahead. We had gotten the rock attention we deserved, but we needed to take this into a new foreign land for the Patti Smith Group. We had to go for airplay at Top 40 radio. It became my mission to make it happen.

Rick Sklar, the toughest program director in the world, had moved up the corporate ladder and his handpicked guy, Glenn Morgan, was now in charge of WABC.

Thankfully, Glenn and I got along great. Glenn was young, well dressed, open to new music, and loved to socialize. He wasn't married.

Patti's record was climbing the charts and the wall I had in front of me was high, but I was going to work him as hard as I could to gain his trust with me.

One time I brought Melissa Manchester over to his office late in the afternoon and things went so well Glenn said, "Lets hang out!" We got a limo, headed to Glenn's East Side apartment and then go out to a hip, cool restaurant like Elaine's or Maxwell's Plum.

When we had a party for Barry Manilow on the roof of the St. Regis Hotel I made sure Glenn got in the Clive Davis/ Barry pictures that would be distributed to the press outlets. I made sure the gossip gal at the Daily News wrote Glenn's name into the column the next day, then I would frame the story and the photograph for him to hang at home.

Glenn was young and full of enthusiasm. My kind of guy! Although he didn't participate in the CBGB's lower east side scene, I made sure he knew all about the Patti Smith Group, Blondie, Television and the Ramones.

On June 6, 1978, WABC added "Because the Night." It was an historic moment for me.

WABC had Andy Gibb at #1, Johnny Mathis with Deniece Williams was #2 and Olivia Newton-John was #3.

The Patti Smith Group came on the chart higher than the new Abba, "Take a Chance on Me," record! WABC was still not playing "This Time I'm in it for Love," by Player, which was a Top 10 record in Billboard.

When I heard the great news WABC added "Because the Night," I told my boss who immediately called Clive. While he was on the phone with him he said, "David's right here," and then put Clive on the speakerphone. Obviously, I was expecting him to say congratulations, but he said, "David, I don't want you to lose sight on the new, must break singles from John Miles and Austin Roberts. The John Miles is hot and a winner, and just listen to the Austin Roberts record and you'll know."

I said, "Clive, getting the Patti Smith Group or any other record on WABC is just the beginning. It's where my job starts. We need store reports and requests. We need a huge push this week from everyone to close the big stations. WABC is watching us and we need to deliver. They really stepped out of the box for us on this one. We must deliver a hit!"

When I was done he said to my boss, "Take me off the speaker and pick up the phone."

45 RPM (Recollections Per Minute)

I went to my office and let the sales people know we had a first. People were parading by high-fiving me. The high you get from promoting a record was at a peak level.

At the artist level, you wonder if and how they find out if their record is on the air. Those calls weren't my responsibility.

On July 9th, the Patti Smith Group played Central Park. I hadn't seen Clive in weeks and I was standing backstage and saw him walking towards me. I knew he'd stop and shake hands but he just kept on going.

For Arista's history as a label, "Because the Night," wasn't a national smash. It was a New York City hit. Arista couldn't crack the Top 10 and it stalled at #13 in Billboard and with a great single leading the way, the album, "Easter," peaked at #20.

Chapter 26
The New Wonder Of The World

The music director at WNEW FM called me giggling. He said, "What's with all the hype?" He was speaking about an ad for an Alan Parsons Project record that was coming out.

I told him it's the way they do things around here. Soon all the key tastemakers in New York were laughing at the hyped up ads that were a consistent part of the Arista marketing machine.

This new ad was expensive and made us all look ridiculous.

"THE NEW WONDER OF THE WORLD" read the full color, two page ad in Billboard on June 24th.

"From the creators of the rock masterpiece, "I Robot," comes one of the most spectacular albums ever recorded! – "Pyramid" by the Alan Parsons Project."

This hype sounded silly and was way over the top.

Clive decided to play back the entire album in a hotel ballroom with all the key NY tastemakers. We had to deliver top people for this historic record. I begged everyone to come. At the event it was clear Clive was no Walt Disney or P.T. Barnum. There were no drinks served and Clive was hiding himself from meeting any of the people that had come. The lights went off and you could feel the cold air-conditioning blowing. Then Clive went up to the podium and began to talk about the record. The first thing you notice is your ass hurts from sitting so long. Then you realize the music isn't great. Then it becomes clear the music is too loud. When the first song ended, we didn't know what to do. Do we clap? Do we cheer? Do we throw our fists up? Clive decided it was time to play the same song over again. And again. We all had a headache and there was no way to leave. He would torture us for another hour. Listening to Clive present music is an awful experience. His presentation is dry and cold. It always ended with "We have another masterpiece!" It just wasn't believable.

WNEW FM added it out of the box along with the Rolling Stones' "Some Girls" and Bruce Springsteen's "Darkness On The Edge Of Town."

In June of '78, the Rolling Stones were on tour playing small club dates including Passaic's Capitol Theater, and Bruce was also on tour and playing local gigs. Getting tickets to any of these shows was tough due to overwhelming demand.

The Rolling Stones single, "Miss You," was on everyone's radio that summer and Bruce was on fire and selling out large arenas.

For Parsons, we knew nothing of what this "project" was about. There was no tour, no photographs and no interviews were forthcoming. We had nothing to work with.

The hype was too strong. Everyone knew this wasn't as good as Pink Floyd, and the past Parsons Projects' records weren't getting any recurrent airplay like Pink Floyd's "Dark Side of the Moon."

Clive wouldn't let you out of the room until he could see the loyalty in your eyes that you would present this as a masterpiece. I knew we had a problem. He was full of shit.

WNEW played it in heavy rotation and even reported that to the trades. But it wasn't selling like the Bruce Springsteen or the Rolling Stones, so Clive starting writing to the sales manager about the Parsons being in heavy rotation, but not selling enough.

The sales manager would complain he wasn't hearing it every hour and so the heavy rotation that was being reported must be hype.

This attitude was awful. Sales and promotion need to get along and not have the president of the company pestering the pros. It was never like this at WB, RCA, or anywhere else I worked.

The Parsons Project lacked soul, depth, and emotion and no matter what Clive said, the album was never going down in history as memorable. As a matter of fact, over the past 18 years since they kept a record of airplay, this Parsons Project disc has gotten less than 40 spins in all of the U.S.A.

By the middle of July, the Alan Parsons Project failed to crack the Top 40 album chart.

When it was clear the Parsons Project wasn't going to be the new wonder of the world, Clive immediately changed course. He wrote the staff a letter that began:

"I'm concerned that all of our attention will go to the Alan Parsons album at the outset and that the Michael

Stanley Band album will not get it's just due. I am reminded of how a well-oiled promotion blitz can suck radio into its own blitz. I know Alan Parsons will get explosive results but are we doing the necessary drumbeating for the Stanley Band album?"

The Michael Stanley Band's album, "Cabin Fever," was a stiff too. It peaked at #99 on the Top 100 Billboard albums chart. Funny to note, Clive took co-production credit on this monster bomb. Of course Clive didn't like what the band turned in and decided he knew how to make it better. I can't make this stuff up.

90 days after the Parsons debacle was released, Clive was still hell bent on turning it around. Although he met the WNEW FM DJ's when he previewed the album back on June 1, he wrote to me: "I know it's somewhat late to get into this, but where a station initially doubts an albums viability, we've got to come back and fight for it. If WNEW didn't believe in Parsons at the outset, we certainly deserve more support for this brilliant creative artist."

Clive was beating a dead horse. Besides, my immediate boss never got on my case or sent me any notes about the record. He understood the score.

The single from the album was called "What Goes Up" and it failed miserably, peaking at #87 on the Billboard singles chart.

Six months later, after heavy play on WNEW FM, the Parsons album failed to reach the year end Top 25 albums that was voted on by the listeners of the station.

At WPLJ – 95.5, another New York rock radio station, they sent out a list of the Top 95 albums of the year. The

45 RPM (Recollections Per Minute)

list was determined from retail record sales in the New York metropolitan area. The Alan Parsons Project failed to make the list.

To this day, nobody plays it or remembers it.

Chapter 27
1978 – Duly Noted

June '78, I was six months into my new job at Arista and instead of summer hits, the label was cold as ice. It was embarrassing. Arista couldn't score nationally with "Because the Night" by the Patti Smith Group. Even though we were early on WABC and moving up, the record stalled at #13 for three weeks in a row. That means it's over and won't go Top 10 due to lack of support. Barry Manilow's track, "Even Now," stalled and was #19 for two weeks running. It had run its course and wouldn't go into the Top 10 either.

Meanwhile, Clive wanted us to chase our tails with a new single by Kevin Lamb and a new Strawbs single. He wrote, "It's time now to take the wraps off and really go after the Kevin Lamb record. The reaction wherever it's played is so strong that we <u>know</u> we have an absolute winner."

The Kevin Lamb song was called "On the Wrong Track" and it was an absolute bomb. It came on Billboard at #87 and took a weak jump to #84 without a bullet. It was the kiss of death for any radio station to be interested.

Kevin Lamb, with all the noise at the top of the mountain, all the money and commitment from the top dogs, couldn't break. It was a frosty reception for this priority single. Radio wasn't interested in playing it.

The Strawbs didn't chart at all.

Like I said, Arista was cold.

Clive ended his note with the "must break" singles. The first song was by John Miles called "I've Never Been In Love Before." Clive said, "It's hot and a winner." And Austin Roberts "Baby, I'm On Fire." Both were stiffs.

Like I said, Arista was cold.

Getting hits played early or on time is a chore, but getting unknown songs by unknown artists at the Top 40 stations to be interested, was out of the question.

July 17 we all got a memorandum from the Midas Man. This time he was highlighting his new approach. "Arista is immediately poised to become a real power in the field of rhythm and blues."

"And it's now ALL UP TO YOU!"

It went on to say, "With our forthcoming artists and product, we could and should have the majority of the entire Top 10 to ourselves."

Clive went on to pontificate about the new product:

Michael Henderson's new record, "In the Night Time." (The album featured two singles, "In the Night Time" and "Take Me I'm Yours." They both bombed at Pop radio, never making the Top 75.)

Norman Connors' new record, "This Is Your Life." (This song also bombed at Pop radio and wasn't even a Top 30 R&B single.)

45 RPM (Recollections Per Minute)

Eddie Kendricks' new single, "The Best of Strangers Now." (Another bomb at Pop radio and wasn't even a Top 30 R&B single.)

Clive mentioned a group called The Quazar, which turned out to be another band without any success.

Clive's note to the staff continued: "The Afro Cuban Band has a smash. This is a crossover R&B hit and should break out of the gate! And don't forget the single from Gladys Knight and the Pips, "Come Back and Finish What You Started." This record is hot from beginning to end. Just listen and you'll know Top 40 doesn't have to wait for R&B and disco."

The Afro Cuban band didn't break out of the gate and Gladys Knight and the Pips was a stiff single.

He ended the note with this line: "I don't know what your work habits have been in the past, but we need organization, discipline, coordination, dedication, and energy to bring ALL these records to the top. What's more, you'll need chutzpah to demand triple adds at key stations."

I was getting a headache and beginning to hear his voice when I read his memos.

While Arista was squeezing out sparks, nothing was igniting. When things don't go the way the boss wants them to go, the tempers flare and the finger pointing begins. When I worked at WB, I never got notes from my boss or the president of the company. If they stopped by the office, the only thing they'd say is, "Why isn't the music louder?" It was the very best of times.

My direct boss at Arista was cool and he gave me a great performance review that said:

Dave Morrell

"Dave has been instrumental in developing the New York market in terms of strengthening Arista's promotion and establishing key relationships at both the radio and retail level. He accepts responsibility, is open to direction, and works hard.

Dave works very well with the national trade representative in New York and has achieved key reviews of Arista single and album product. He is loyal and dependable, initiating projects and successfully following them through.

To his credit WABC has played more Arista product then ever before, i.e. Raydio, John Williams, Patti Smith Group, several Barry Manilow selections.

Dave's potential for growth at Arista Record's is excellent. He is held in high regard."

Chapter 28
The Promotion Man

What is a promotion man?

In 1975, Cash Box magazine presented an editorial called, "Adding Life to the Business," which stated:

"Being a promotion man is perhaps the toughest and most demanding, yet one of the most rewarding positions that an individual can have in the record industry. The A&R department can find the best talent, sign the group, record them, produce their record, manufacture it and put a few thousand copies out on the street. Then it's up to the promotion man to get the record played. Sometimes he does. More often than not, he doesn't.

Yet it's not his fault. Stations are tightening up, playing maybe the Top 25 records. Indeed Top 40 is a thing of the past.

Even records that are Top 10 are only now being added at some major stations and some stations begin to play records as they start to fall off the charts. Who is blamed? The promotion man, of course. For him the revolting fact is that he has no control over the people who control his destiny.

Perhaps the promotion man's position is similar to that of a manager or coach in organized sports. If the team fails or falters, you can't fire the whole team, the president or the general manager. You fire the coach or manager. It's the same in the record industry. If a number of records on a label stiff out, it's got to be the promotion man's fault, so get rid of him. It couldn't possibly be the fault of the president or vice president, A&R, marketing, merchandising or sales departments.

Surprisingly, though, even with the cards apparently stacked against them, promotion men tell us they wouldn't trade their jobs for any other at the record company level. They enjoy and love the challenge of being out on the streets, encouraging, demanding, pleading, cajoling, bargaining, arguing or coaxing recalcitrant music directors into playing their records. They keep the industry going and they love it. They add an extraordinary amount of life and vitality to an exciting business, that might be as exciting as the shoe business, if they weren't around.

Cash Box applauds the promotion man. He's a one of a kind individual."

In January of '79, Billboard ran a story about executives that came from promotion. It was called, "Label Leaders Culled From Promotion Ranks" and written by Irv Lichtman.

The article reported that the top executives in the music business came from a promotion background. The list of top people includes Joe Smith, Jerry Moss, Ron Alexenburg, Neil Bogart, Steve Popovich and Dick Klein, just to name a few.

Joe Smith was the President of WB when I worked there and I'd work with him again at Capitol Records in the 80's. Joe said, "The music industry is more than the table manufacturing business. Promotion is where the top executives of this business should come from. Their familiarity with radio and music trends is of extraordinary value. Elements of blue-sky optimism and certainly the most enthusiasm. They have the ability to come back from setbacks. You can learn accounting, you can hire lawyers, but it takes a marvelous street feeling to gain a sense of what's a hit record and how to get it played."

Dick Klein, executive vice president of Polydor, says, "The promotion man is the most natural person to turn to. He is the one attuned to radio and to what the public demands. It's on-the-job training for meeting people head on and street trained pros are best suited to do so."

Some people think the promotion man has a restricted outlook on music but it's not true. Ron Alexenburg said, "It was the promotion man who invented the concept of crossover records. Promotion men share a street-smart sense in not taking no for an answer, having a self-starting ability, anticipating a problem with a 'what if' contingency approach and enormous ambition. In planning, plotting, scheming, nurturing, each promotion man has his own style."

Ron went on to say, "Out of a total of 40 people at my company, 29 are in promotion."

Steve Popovich, President of Cleveland International Records, currently riding high with Meatloaf said, "Promotion men are self–motivated people who prefer giving direction and making things happen."

Mike Klenfner, senior vice president and assistant to the president of Atlantic Records says, "Promotion folks can make top level executives because of their ability to adjust themselves to quickly changing situations with regard to a records radio life. You can work the same record in many different ways."

Clive Davis, on the other hand, prior to joining Columbia, served three years with the law firm of Rosenman, Colin, Cotin, Kaye, Petscheck & Freund. While there, Clive devoted his talents to general corporate matters. When asked why Columbia Records had a predominance of lawyers in its key executive positions he said "Perhaps the study of law tends to discipline the mind without stifling creativity and thereby serve as ideal basic training for an executive."

Chapter 29
"Don't Cry Out Loud" – Melissa Manchester

On October 28th, I got a letter in the mail from an artist and new friend, Melissa Manchester. It read:

Dave,

"Thanks for whisking us through the New York scene - high and smiling. Hope to see you in LA or NY."

Love, Melissa

Melissa was the greatest woman I worked with. She was Marlo Thomas and Mary Tyler Moore rolled into one big happy smile. I'd walk over hot coals for her.

When it came to setting up a record where the artist was 100% committed like Melissa, I could set my sights high and work out a radio plan that could succeed.

The song was called "Don't Cry Out Loud."

Melissa had roots in New York City as a performer and knew her way around town. This made it tough. I knew she had her own relationships with some key DJ's so I made sure everyone got a copy of the record so nobody would complain to her.

I put together a campaign with a budget and showed it to my boss. He signed off and I spent the rest of the week putting the plan into effect.

I did a recap of events in a letter to my boss on November 27th. It went like this:

On Monday, October 23rd, when Melissa came to New York, "Don't Cry Out Loud" had just been released. At that time the following schedule was in place:

    10:30 – WNEW-AM/FM
    11:00 – WNBC/Y97
    12:00 – WCBS-FM
    2:00 – WPIX-FM
    3:00 – WABC

Aside from meeting each Program Director and Music Director, Melissa also met with the various disc jockeys that were on the air at the time. This list included Ted Brown from WNEW-AM, Pete Fornatale from WNEW-FM and Dan Ingram at WABC.

Melissa concluded this radio promotion tour by writing a brief note to everyone she met, which we would deliver with each album in two weeks time.

This past Monday, November 20th, Melissa came back to another day of promotional activities.

    Lunch with the following tastemakers:
    Alpha Distributers salesman
    WNEW-AM - Music Director
    WCBS-FM - Music Director
    WRNW – Music Director
    WLIR-FM – Music Director

45 RPM (Recollections Per Minute)

2:00 – WDHA (Dover, NJ.) phone interview (contest on air to tie in with all New Jersey Harmony Hut stores.
2:30 – Record World Magazine interview.
3:30 – WGHQ (Kingston NY) phone interview. Station moved "Don't Cry Out Loud" from #19 t0 #17 this week.
5:30 – Melissa, Pam (road manager) and I met with Glenn Morgan, WABC Program Director, to have a drink.
7:30 – Glenn Morgan invited Melissa, Pam and myself to his apartment to relax before going out to dinner.
9:30 – On Melissa's request, we decided to see a show and have dinner at Michael's Pub where Woody Allen performed. A great time was had by all.
As you can see, Melissa has made significant gains with radio people she had only met with briefly on past occasions. As "Don't Cry Out Loud" continues to gain in the pop charts, it is apparent we should be early in collecting airplay in the New York market.

"Don't Cry Out Loud" was the fastest rising chart single of her career.

I didn't mention in my note that we also smoked pot thanks to Glenn Morgan at WABC. When I offered up a smoke he said he wasn't allowed to partake due to legal situations, but he said it was okay if we smoked HIS pot. Guess what? We did.

The only time I saw Melissa upset was when she told the story of "Don't Cry Out Loud." It was a song by Peter Allen that Clive wanted her to do. She didn't want to do it. She felt the message was against who she was. She told me she even called Bob Dylan to talk about the jam she was in. "What would he do?" she said. She knew if she didn't do it she'd face the wrath of Clive, but if she did it, she'd get the priority she needed for her career so she cut the song.

Arista big wigs decided to follow up Melissa's hit with a song called "Through the Eyes Of Love" from the movie "Ice Castles," rather than a second track from this recent album. The choice was horrible. The song was a stiff and didn't make the Top 75 in Billboard. It put an end to any sales on this current record.

It was October when we went to work on "Don't Cry Out Loud." By April of the following year, it was still in the Top 15 at WABC.

Melissa did the work. She was the ultimate professional.

I wouldn't have this much fun again until I worked with Donny Osmond on "Soldier Of Love," a #2 hit song in 1989.

Chapter 30
New York City's WNEW FM Top 25 Albums 1978

WNEW FM asked their listeners to write in and vote for their favorite albums of the year. They weren't the top sellers or leaders in the charts. The poll showed the records the audience in New York wanted to hear.

Richard Neer was the DJ at the time and he ran the results on his show January 1, 1979. It was a mild New Year's Day with a light rain and a temperature of 58 degrees.

At #25 was Talking Heads with "More Talk." The previous year Talking Heads were #6 in the survey. At #24 was Heart with "Dog & Butterfly." It was the first time Heart made the Top 25. At #23 was Genesis and their album "Then There Were Three." At #22 was "Tormato" by Yes. At #21 was new artist, Nick Lowe, whose UK album, "The Jesus of Cool," was changed in America to, "Pure Pop for Now People." Nick was a new artist and on the survey for the first time with his debut album.

At #20 was Cheap Trick with "Heaven Tonight." At #19 was Dan Fogelberg and Tim Weisberg's, "Twin Sons of Different Mothers." At #18, for the first time on the survey, was Blondie with "Parallel Lines."

Among the best new artists on the list were the Blues Brothers, Dire Straits, Steve Forbert, Devo, Kate Bush and George Thorogood.

At #17 was Jackson Browne with "Running on Empty." At #16 was Neil Young with "Come a Time," and at #15 was the Tom Robinson Band with "Motorway."

Arista had the #14 record with "Shakedown Street" by the Grateful Dead and the #13 record with "Misfits" by the Kinks. The Kinks had a loyal following so it was odd they made the list for the first time. Van Morrison came in at #11 with his album "Wavelength."

At #10 was the group Renaissance with "Song For All Seasons." At #9, were the Cars, considered the best new group of the year, with "Just What I Needed." Tied with the Cars at #9 was Bob Dylan and his album "Street Legal."

Arista had the #8 record with "Easter" by the Patti Smith Group.

At #7 was Bob Seger and the Silver Bullet Band with "Stranger in Town." At #6 was Southside Johnny's "Hearts of Stone."

At #5 was Elvis Costello with "This Year's Model." At #4 was the Who's, "Who Are You." At #3 was "52nd Street" by Billy Joel. At #2 was the Rolling Stones "Some Girls." And finally, at #1, was "Darkness on the Edge of Town" by Bruce Springsteen and the E Street Band.

45 RPM (Recollections Per Minute)

The radio never sounded so good. It had been a great year for me to work some really cool records.

For Alan Parsons Project, after months of heavy airplay, it was clear the radio listener didn't want to hear it again. I rest my case.

Chapter 31
"(Wish I Could Fly Like) Superman" - Kinks

In late January of '79 the mail arrived with a package from the U.K. that had all the international releases from Arista. I got on that list and would hunt for records that would fit Scott Muni's Friday afternoon show on WNEW FM called "Things From England."

To my surprise, there was a new Kinks record. It was called "(Wish I Could Fly Like) Superman." I loved the Kinks so I immediately dropped the needle and knew I had to get this over to Scott pronto. It just happened to be a Friday, too.

When I got down to the station around noon, Scott was in a great mood when I handed him the record. He played it in his office and loved it. He said he'd give it a World Premier with a big buildup. It was exactly what I had hoped for!

I got back to the office and told everyone to turn the radio up when the Kinks came on! It's a wonderful feeling to dig a record and be in the home office when everyone else is hearing it on the radio for the first time.

It sounded great on the air and everyone was gassed up.

Later that evening, the DJ that followed Scott called me and told me he was going to play it, too. I was thrilled!

By Monday, the whole radio staff at WNEW FM was into it and the import was getting heavy airplay.

"(Wish I Could Fly Like) Superman" was rush released as an American single in March and ended up a stiff, not making it into the Top 40 singles list in Billboard.

Arista dropped the ball on this great single.

"Low Budget," the album that contained the single, came out in July.

The Kinks following was so strong in New York we had no trouble getting support from radio. WPLJ added "(Wish I Could Fly Like) Superman" before there was stock in the stores! Over at WNEW FM, the morning man got 61 calls to play the record!

The Kinks single was reacting like a hit! New York, The Gotham city, was loving Superman!

Chapter 32
1979 – Nitty Gritty

We headed to Puerto Rico for a company meeting in the dead of winter. It was cold in New York and hot in the 51st state. The first night it was warm and balmy and the pool was calling us.

Clive had a welcome address that was 45 minutes too long and during it he mentioned a movie he brought down for us to see 'if we wanted to' in his suite called "Ice Castles." Speaking for myself, I wanted nothing to do with the word ICE, so I boohooed the invite. Besides, the movie was about a champion ice skater whose hopes were dashed when she was stricken blind.

Nobody wanted to see it.

We all headed to the pool and overtook the stereo system. We were letting off steam and loving it. I doubt if any one of us went to bed before 5am.

Then we woke up to the sound of Clive huffing and puffing down the hallway pushing his peon's around while grunting. He was steamed.

We all headed into a dark, dank, cold ballroom and Clive took to the stage.

He was at the lectern coughing, touching the microphone, and getting ready for the kill. He went into a tirade about nobody coming to watch "Ice Castles" after he brought it all the way from New York, "special," just for us to witness this incredible movie with an unbelievable soundtrack.

He talked for 45 minutes, beating us down and making us all feel crummy.

For his speech and presentation of new product there was no charm and no soul. He sounded like a lawyer trying to sell us on the potential. He'd talk up the act as though it would be bigger than the Beatles and we could all be making history.

After the boasting, it would be a semester on the songwriters, the producers, the order of the songs on an album and then he would play the so-called hit. Then he talked about his expectations and what he's observed about other artists in the elk. Then he'd play it again, and again, and again. After four times, he'd move to the second focus track, then he'd play a few more tracks, before returning to the single AGAIN.

It was painful and 99% of what we heard was stiffs.

We came back from warm and beautiful Puerto Rico to another chilly winter.

The Billboard charts in January told the story itself. Arista was ice cold. They had no singles in the Top 25. It was dreary on the album side, too. Besides Manilow's "Greatest Hits," we had no other album in the Top 40. Arista had a great staff of promo pro's, but the product was so poor they couldn't get anything to stick.

45 RPM (Recollections Per Minute)

We kicked off the New Year with new singles from Al Stewart, "Song on the Radio," and Eric Carmen's remake of "Baby, I Need Your Lovin'." Neither of them made the Top 25. On the album front, we had stinkers from Andy Mendelson, Camel, Dwight Twilly and Angie Bofill.

In March, Clive wrote the following note to the promotion staff:

"TnT now stands for Tycoon and Twilly. The action is feverish and it is exciting, to say the least. Also, the response to the pre-release interest in Robert Fleishman is overwhelming. But don't forget Graham Parker. His debut album for Arista is piercing, brilliant, tough and exceptional in every way.

Elvis Costello currently has the #10 album in the country without a hit single. Graham Parker's album is stronger and more vital. This album should be one of the top albums of the year."

By year's end, it didn't even make the Top 25 countdown on WNEW FM, although Elvis Costello was in the Top 5.

This is the time Clive went ape-shit about this year's Alan Parsons Project. He gave the promotion staff a pounding over it. You could feel the hot air coming at you. Your head hurt from the loud volume of the hype. We'd be told to eat, shit and fuck Parsons. We were told nothing was more important, not you're family or your personal time.

Clive's campaign for the Alan Parsons Project album called "Eve" went like this:

"The new work of a genius! From a man who does the impossible! Now comes "Eve," a dazzling musical vision from the only man that could give it life!"

131

Dave Morrell

The esteemed rock writer, Robert Christgau, wrote, "This is schlock that knows its name. Thematically, it's both sophomoric and disgusting. Visually, it's sadistic. What is it they stencil on street corners? Castrate art-rockers?" He gave "Eve" a D.

The head honcho, president and his weak underlings could not get anything going, so what happens then? They fired the VP of rock promotion.

A few days later the Executive Vice President and General Manager wrote me note with a cute little curly-cue signature at the end of it.

"Dear Dave, The fiscal year that ended June 30, 1979 was a difficult one for Arista Records. The last half of the year saw the impact on sales and particularly profits of the flattening of the market. A greater effort will be required to continue our achievement under difficult conditions."

Arista was frozen with no direction from the top that could pull us out. A&R was terrible, the marketing hype was awful on each record. Careers weren't being built. If you were young and full of enthusiasm, Arista wasn't the place to be.

By the end of August, we got another hit on the head from upstairs. Clive wrote us all a note that said, "It's vital we come out of the box with a strong week on the Alan Parsons single. It is common for artists with a strong rock record to bullet strongly on to the Top 40 charts. We've got to do it with Alan Parsons. We need major stations and key adds immediately. (Then, out of nowhere, he ended the note with) P.S. Don't forget the new A's single."

Parsons wasn't a hit single. The A's didn't have a hit single. Clive was pulling at straws. The A's were a punk band and it was stupid to even put out a single that nobody wanted to play. They didn't care for the album either.

To kick off the year we were ice cold and now, in late July, Arista was still frozen out with everything Clive brought to the market.

In Billboard (July 21) we only had one song in the Top 40 called "You Can't Change That" by Raydio. On the album side, Arista had no albums in the Top 40. It was grim and Clive began the campaign to be rid of the field promotion staff that he blamed for not getting his stiffs played on the radio.

I'd get notes out of the blue on dumb shit from Clive. Arista had a band they were having trouble launching. They were going to call it "Cash" but changed it to "Tycoon." Clive wrote to me, "New York group, hit album, hit single….and a great intro for commercials." The album never made the Top 40. The band never toured and there was no one in the band anyone ever heard of. This was the crap I had to deal with from the highest levels. Clive was feeding us stiffs.

Here's another example of his bluster. Clive wrote a note to me that said, "Considering the WABC format and Glenn Morgan's desire for breaking records, please go after the Stewart Thomas Group's record as a priority for WABC."

For starters, the WABC format was the toughest in the country and was never the place to break records. Clive's comment was way out of line and Glenn Morgan never had such intentions to break records. He played it safe with few songs and huge ratings. The song Clive was writing about was called "To Freak or Not to Freak." It was a stiff with no story, nothing, nada. It was another annoying note. I wondered why my direct boss wasn't mentioning anything to me and if other promotion people were getting these buzz kill notes from the top.

The label had money to spend, but Clive wasn't scoring anything new and interesting. When this happens, he beats you over the head and makes you feel you haven't got the relationships needed to get records played on the radio.

Come October, and Clive was beating the bones of what was once a dead horse. He wouldn't stop with Alan Parsons so he wrote another note that read:

"We really must improve the airplay rotation on Parsons where it's just fair. The album's chart strength is overpowering. It's the third or fourth best selling rock album in the country. (Actually, ahead of it in sales were Led Zeppelin, The Eagles, Styx, Foreigner, Cheap Trick, The Knack, Supertramp and Neil Young and Crazy Horse, just to show you how off Clive was with his stats.) You've got an ad in the new Radio & Records that all the lagging stations should see. You've got to do better in the East on Parsons."

In November another note arrived from Clive. This time, instead of pushing for airplay, he just wanted to get his records reviewed in the trades. Each week the trades got over 150 singles and he wanted personal attention on two more upcoming stiffs. He wrote: "Make sure the Twilly and Walsh singles are specifically brought to Billboard's and Record World's attention for review this week. Without a previous sales history, I know it's hard."

I should have told him that it was my experience that programmers don't add records from seeing ads or reviews. It took sales and requests, but I knew he wouldn't listen. He knew it all.

45 RPM (Recollections Per Minute)

As we were heading into Christmas, and about to have two weeks off with our family, things got ugly. Arista announced in the December 22 issue of Billboard they were 'restructuring' its staff. Of course, the hard working 24/7 promotion people were all blamed and some were let go. Some top radio people were pissed off.

A key programmer from Portland, Oregon with the #1 Pop station wrote a note to Clive that said:

"I feel I have to comment on the recent dismissal of the Arista promotion man in the Seattle/Northwest area. I know you're busy, so I'll try to be brief. Michael Wright was recently fired and to say I'm upset about this move is an understatement. When I spoke to Michael he said it was sudden and unexpected. The reason he was given was that the promotional duties for Seattle and San Francisco were to be consolidated and Arista felt Michael wasn't strong enough to handle the combined area.

This is nonsense and something somewhere is wrong within Arista. When I was program director at KROY in Sacramento, California, Michael was the Arista man for the Bay area. He was loyal to the label, was in constant touch, and when he promised we'd have support on a marginal add, or a giveaway, he was there.

I have read your recent pronouncements in the trades with great interest especially in view of Michaels sacking.

After a career that spans two complete building jobs at two national labels, and a public stance of high morality and quality, I find it completely and totally inexcusable that a loyal and solid employee could be fired two weeks before

Christmas, and just months after your company moved his family from his base in San Francisco to Seattle.

I'm sure there were lots of good words exchanged and toasts and promises flowed with the announcement of the new job. I was excited by the news and was looking forward to hearing from him again.

So when I heard he was being replaced, and by who, I found it pretty easy to connect the dots and come up with a picture of petty political power move that's better left to companies of less import than Arista.

I understand that when a new regime moves in at any level the spoils go to the victors, but I simply can't believe the executives at Arista cannot condone the cutting of a good employee at such an inopportune time.

Is business so bad that you can't find a position for a loyal employee? Can you justify turning a man from employee to unemployment recipient at the time of year parties and celebrations are being planned? Do you think that moves such as these will endear Arista to the Northwest?

I've heard nothing but negatives during the past several weeks as the word spread. While this letter may not change anything, I want to make damn sure you know how my attitude toward Arista has changed. It can't be changed by big dinners or Christmas gifts given in radio's name to charity.

Mr. Davis, charity begins at home. Michael Wright will find a job and he certainly doesn't need any charity and when Michael gets hooked up with another label and his record and your record are in a toss up on my desk, do I have to tell you who will win?

45 RPM (Recollections Per Minute)

The shaft that Michael Wright got is making me think what has happened to Arista? Where is the dignity? Where is the class?

I hope this letter will make the next man think before he reaches for the 'eject' button!"

Clive waited a month to reply. He wrote back:

"Anything I could say in answer to you, I believe, might fall on an emotionally closed disposition."

Who wants to work for a company that doesn't have your back? Personally, I had to get out of there. There was no air to breathe. I was hoping lightning would strike me.

What else could go wrong for Arista? For starters, Barry Manilow would fall a million units short over the holidays.

The shit storm continued into the New Year.

Barry fell out of the Top 20 with his album and now Arista was starting a new decade with no singles or albums in the Top 20.

Arista had become the Titanic that struck an iceberg.

Chapter 33
"Déjà Vu" – Dionne Warwick

At the end of the year during the big holiday season, Arista had nothing besides Barry Manilow to squawk about. It's all I heard about. The sales team was in a tizzy to sell records. Meanwhile, nobody was mentioning Dionne Warwick, who was coming off a big hit with "I'll Never Love This Way Again."

It was December and everything at radio was winding down for the holidays. WABC was about to announce their final adds before freezing the list and playing Christmas songs.

Barry Manilow was still on the WABC playlist with "Ships" and his album, "One Voice," was a Top 10 album in New York City.

Dionne Warwick was the key record we needed to get on. It was called "Déjà Vu."

It was key to seize on this opportunity at all costs. There would be no way to regain the momentum in January when things started up again. I needed to score.

Isaac Hayes wrote the song and Barry Manilow produced it. It was the follow up single to Dionne's hit, "I'll Never Love This Way Again."

I remember a show she did at Carnegie Hall. It was superb in every way. She was elegant with a great band and the set list included some of my favorite songs of all time. I took a key radio guy and after the show we went back to say hello to Dionne. She was sweet and friendly and a chain smoker. After hanging out for half an hour, we headed out to leave and found ourselves on the stage at Carnegie Hall. When we turned our heads, Barry Manilow was heading our way.

He walked out on to the stage with no audience, spread his arms out and began to wail. We laughed and then Barry told us to watch him throw his voice all around this historic music hall.

We talked and posed for some personal photographs and then stood still as we took in the view a performer would have on this infamous stage. Dionne had walked out and joined us on stage, too. It was a wonderful moment.

At this point, Dionne's record, "Déjà Vu," was back at 38* on Billboard and her album was way back at 78*. It was a stretch for WABC to be looking at it this early since the last single, "I'll Never Love This Way Again," peaked at #9.

We needed a Christmas miracle and we got it!

WABC added it ahead of the national charts at #29 on their playlist!

It had been five long years since we squeezed one on WABC's last playlist of the year. Going all the way back to '74 with "Bungle in the Jungle" by Jethro Tull.

45 RPM (Recollections Per Minute)

"Déjà Vu" was a ballad and went on to win a Grammy in the R&B category. Dionne also won for "I'll Never Fall In Love Again" in the Pop category, making her the first artist to win in both R&B and Pop in the same year.

A year from now (1980), I'd look back to see the results of the WABC Top 100 Songs of the Year. Funny, but besides Air Supply, the only song from Arista on the list was "Déjà Vu" by Dionne Warwick.

141

Chapter 34
The Conference Call "We're A Million Short On Manilow!"

It was the first call of the year. A sales-boss was running it and he was in no mood to ask us how our holidays were. It was time to drill down and it went like this:

"The Manilow album, and this should stay on this conference call, is a million units below what he is capable of. We have to attack every record store, right now, going into every store there is, making sure it's displayed like a brand new album. As we know the album isn't brand new, it's been out for almost four months, but we have to milk it for all it's worth.

"The strategy this week is for the single to take 10 point jumps at every station. It will help us sell records."

The single he's talking about is "Ships," which was a Top 10 single at WABC. The station had been pounding it since early November of the previous year.

I said to myself. He's full of shit. Nobody who's worth anything in the music business is going to ask WABC to jump a record 10 points. Besides, the single was already in the Top 10. I did my job, but he couldn't do his, so he figured if he asked for 10 point jumps and if they didn't come in, he could blame the promotion department. This guy was typical of the people working at Arista.

The call continued.

"In New York, lets go over the Christmas season." The guy barked.

The New York sales guy stood his ground and said, "It didn't move up in rank. We didn't move up from the Top 25 because Pink Floyd came on ahead of us. At large accounts like the Sam Goody chain and the Record World stores we did 300 units the past two weeks, and that's half of what their number one album sold, which was Donna Summer. Other top sellers were Barbra Streisand, The Eagles, Fleetwood Mac, and the No-Nukes album. I'd say the TV spots and the retail sampler we made with Barry didn't work. We couldn't get all the stores to use them."

I was zoning out. It was endless. Nobody I knew got a raise or a bonus over the holidays. My time here was running out. The attitude was terrible. And, to make matters worse, this sales guy didn't even mention the Dionne Warwick single, "Déjà Vu," that was added to WABC in December. WABC loved the record, and it became a Top 10 hit for them. The song went on to win a Grammy for Best Female R&B Vocal Performance.

The final part of the call was to discuss the exciting new product.

45 RPM (Recollections Per Minute)

By now we were all drained of enthusiasm and felt lousy.

The upcoming New Year releases that shipped the following week were all duds. I heard the music and my head hurt. They included artists Lydia Lunch, Cristina, Chuck Cissel, David Wolf, John Madden and D.L. Byron.

It was seriously time to move on down the road.

If Arista was a million short on the Manilow, you can only imagine how dismal the rest of records were selling.

After two years at Arista, I realized I wasn't hearing great songs that popped off the turntable. Arista was colder than an ice castle while I was walking on sunshine with my new job at Capitol Records. And don't it feel good!

Chapter 35
"Hooray For Hollywood!"

It was raining and cold and I was having a bad day. I never had bad days but I made the mistake of thinking ahead and my head began to ache. I was walking from the Arista office over to my hangout to nurse a glass of wine. On the way over, I was feeling so hopeless, I begged to get hit by a strike of lightning to end the misery I was feeling at work.

I walked in the restaurant and the owner had the phone in his ear, but put it aside to greet me. As we shook hands I got a jolt of electricity and then he said, "It's for you!" and he handed me the phone.

To my great surprise it was the call I always wanted to receive. It was Maureen O'Conner from Capitol Records. She was the head of Publicity for Capitol Records based in New York. She had never called me before this moment. I knew her through a music director she had been dating. Capitol Records was right next door to the restaurant and she knew to reach me there.

She said there were new changes at Capitol. She said they had an opening!

She said Capitol needed a regional promotion person that would be based in the New York office and be responsible for Boston and Philadelphia, too. She said I'd get to travel, stay at the best hotels, eat at the finest restaurants and have the greatest seat on earth for all the best concerts!

Maureen told me to stop what I was doing and come over instantly. Capitol was on the sixteenth floor on the southeast corner of 6th Avenue at 56th Street. Dustin Hoffman comes out of the building in a scene from Kramer vs. Kramer.

When I got there we hugged and then she introduced me to the guy running things. He was the district manager. He took me into an executive office that was empty and closed the door. He looked me in the eyes and said, "Do you smoke pot?" I froze. I wanted to lie. I leaned into him and whispered, "Yes."

"Good!" he yelled. "You're in! Can you get to Hollywood tomorrow? I want you to meet your new boss."

I left on a cold rainy gray day and headed to Los Angeles. When I landed a few hours later it was summertime. The sun was bright and warm and the leaves and lawns were green. I hadn't seen color like this in months. It was a perfect day.

I went over to the famous Tower on Vine Street in Hollywood. The building is round and looks like a stack of 45's on a big spindle.

I took the elevator up to meet a guy named Ray Tusken. Ray was the guy I would take direction from. He was running the album department. When we met he didn't say, "Sit down." He said, "Lets go!"

We went out the back of the Tower into the parking lot and there it was. A 1979 Trans-Am! A badass midnight blue

45 RPM (Recollections Per Minute)

400 horsepower with WS6 suspension, Hurst shifter, T-top and wire wheels, imported from Oregon. It was clean, no decals, ridiculously fast and easy to get a killer sound from four coaxial speakers and just 100 watts. This was a motherfucker sound that would get many records played on KMET, the #1 rock station in Los Angeles.

Ray made my day, month and year all in a few hours.

The car was so special he wouldn't even let his girlfriend start it!

Ray wanted me to get acquainted with all the new releases. We drove all around, up and down those Hollywood hills, while Ray told me every ingredient to every record we were listening too.

It had been years since I met anyone like Ray.

Capitol was my home for the next 10 years.

We had hits with Paul McCartney, Tina Turner, Duran Duran, Bob Seger, Crowded House, Heart, Queen, Joe Cocker, MC Hammer, Iron Maiden and many more.

To be continued.

The Morrell Archives Volume 4 – Capitol Records 1980 - 1990

Sources:

1. Phil Spector — Sonny Bono "And the Beat Goes On" 1991
2. Arista — Clive Davis - Billboard (August 14, 1965 page 6)
   Rick Sklar – Rocking America: An Insider's Story 1985
   Clive Davis – Inside the Record Business 1975
   Clive Davis – The Soundtrack of My Life 2013
3. WABC — Rick Sklar – Rocking America: An Insider's Story 1985
4. The New Wonder of the World — "New Wonder of the World" Billboard June 24 1978
5. The Promotion Man — 1975 Cash Box Editorial
   1979 Billboard January
6. New York City's WNEW FM Top 25 Albums of 1978 - WNEW FM — Richard Neer
7. 1979 – Nitty Gritty — Rock Albums of the 70's: A Critical Guide - Robert Christgau

Made in the USA
Middletown, DE
24 August 2017